"This is a striking book. I've read  James Lowry does well the work of to meet and be moved by the people deeply moving, the language is poetic, and the biblical reflections are insightful and eye-opening. Never before have so many passages leapt out and encouraged me." **Jay O'Callahan,** storyteller, performer, writer, and workshop leader, Marshfield, MA

"James Lowry brings a poetic vision to his sermons, each of which stands as a well-written wisdom tale drawn from the rich tradition of Southern storytelling. He brings an enlightened heart to his readings of biblical passages, and a writer's eye to the stories of the everyday lives of ordinary people. Readers will be reminded of the oracular strength evident in the work of Peter Gomes, as well as the more earthy insights of cross-genre writers like Kathleen Norris." **Bernie McDonough,** buyer, Elliott Bay Book Company, Seattle

"I've seen men and women moved to tears when Jim Lowry is preaching. He starts with ancient truth, wraps it in homespun stories, and sends it straight to the heart. Jim is not merely among today's best preachers. He is the Poet Laureate for hungry souls." **Ronald Cole-Turner,** Pittsburgh Theological Seminary

"Jim Lowry is a remarkable preacher who brings together a biblical text and a tradition of Southern storytelling. I regularly read his sermons as a part of my devotions." **Erskine Clarke,** editor, *Journal for Preachers*

# Low-Back, Ladder-Back, Cane-Bottom Chair

## BIBLICAL MEDITATIONS

James S. Lowry

With a Foreword by Walter Brueggemann

Saint Mary's Press
Christian Brothers Publications
Winona, Minnesota

Genuine recycled paper with 10% post-consumer waste. Printed with soy-based ink.

The publishing team included Michael Wilt, development editor; Rebecca Fairbank, copy editor; Lynn Dahdal, production editor and typesetter; Stephan Nagel, cover designer; Beth Moore, cover photographer; pre-press, printing, and binding by the graphics division of Saint Mary's Press.

*For Martha*

# Contents

# Foreword

Ours is indeed a *thin* time: our pursuit of the most recent product, our excessive attentiveness to the sound bite, our readiness to throw away everything quickly—heirlooms, people, utterance—our reliance upon can-do technology as a replacement for human attentiveness, all produce thinness. The outcome is predictably a society that ceases to care, a society with little memory and less anticipation, a society eaten deeply by anxiety, unembarrassed about greed, capable of endless euphemisms for brutality. The thinness is a consequence common to conservatives and liberals.

Those of us entrusted with memory and speech wonder about utterance that could veto thinness. More specifically, those of us in the church wonder about preaching as an antidote to thinness, wherein preaching can generate rhetorical thickness that gives place and rootage and belonging and energy for fresh imagination. In this book, wonderment about utterance in general and preaching in particular come down to James Lowry—preacher, craftsman, poet, storyteller, word artist.

In the sermons and tales offered here, Lowry demonstrates his remarkable capacity for *thick speech* that may indeed override our thin antihumanness and evoke a community capable of rooted, energetic humanness. In his use of the term *thick*, Clifford Geertz spoke of culture as life in and by a web of deeply coded utterances and gestures (word and sacrament) that are known, understood, trusted, and cared for by the community. Lowry's preaching is precisely such *a web of deeply coded gestures and utterances.* He moves easily and readily from biblical text to old family tale to rich cultural reflex and back to the text. He does not compromise scriptural authority, but links that textual authority with other textual authorities that live in the recesses of subculture. Lowry has a keen sense for the right word at the right place in the sentence, a right placing that weaves midst the listeners a place of truth, a summons to justice, an offer of love, a risk of honesty, and a wonder of healing.

This book may be read with a double focus. It may be read as a model for preaching. I expect other preachers, would-be preachers, and folk who love to listen will be energized and empowered for that work. But while we are instructed by the models, we will at the same time, without our agreeing, be drawn into the concreteness of delicate utterance, and will find the concreteness lingering as we come to the new places that Lowry makes familiar to us.

In a book on preaching, I used Walt Whitman's fine phrase, "Finally comes the poet." At that time I did not know that one of Whitman's reference points is Lowry. He is a poet. He has been here a while. Here he finally comes to print.

The powers of thinness are powerful among us, committed to narcissism, quick profits, promiscuous economics, and endless self-indulgence. Lowry and folks like him, however, regularly convene the community of *anti-thinness,* where we embrace yet again webbed humanness marked by staggering gifts and stunning demands. Thinness knows nothing of demand and less of gift. But Lowry does, and he invites us in compelling ways to that different humanness that is our treasured birthright and our enduring burden.

WALTER BRUEGGEMANN
Columbia Theological Seminary
January 1999

# Author's Acknowledgments

The narrative details of the family tales in the pieces that follow are true to the best of my memory. I readily confess, however, that the role of memory and the tricks memory plays in the fashioning of narrative make for a mystery that evades me. Except for an occasional nod at poetic license, I have not consciously misrepresented facts. Nevertheless, I must acknowledge gratitude for the patience of my brothers, Bright A. Lowry and M. Banks Lowry, who might remember events with slightly different slants. In my defense, I am sure they will know well that we are not the first in our family to tell tales with differing details. At some important level, all versions are true.

To the other characters in the various stories, I hope I have sufficiently disguised your identity by changing your names and, in some instances, your locale. If I failed, I beg your forgiveness.

Ellis Oakes was my pastor during the most formative years of my life. The careful and serious attention he gave to interpretation of texts in his preaching, and to his devotion to his whole flock, including me, came together to form an example that has stood the test of time. In the well-deserved leisure of his retirement, I want him to know of the esteem in which I hold him.

I have been inspired and informed by the church and wish especially to thank those congregations who have done me the honor of allowing me to be their pastor while I practiced my art. The Church of the Good Shepherd (Presbyterian) in Anniston, Alabama; the First Presbyterian Church of Marianna, Florida; the Orange Park Presbyterian Church near Jacksonville, Florida; the Mount Pleasant Presbyterian Church near Charleston, South Carolina; and the Idlewild Presbyterian Church of Memphis, Tennessee, at various times, have been both family and fellow travelers. I am grateful.

Without the encouragement of Professor Walter Brueggemann, this project would never have had a beginning. His foreword is full of grace. I am grateful more than I can say, and I'm honored by his confidence. I am likewise grateful to Professor Brueggemann's colleague at Columbia Theological Seminary and my friend since high school, Professor Erskine Clarke. In this project, as in other matters both personal and professional, he is a great source of encouragement.

Ted Wardlaw, my friend and colleague at Central Presbyterian Church in Atlanta, was gracious in remembering the line from one of my sermons that became the title of this book. I do not take such friendship for granted.

In more concrete ways, I am grateful to Retha Moore, my administrative assistant on the staff of Idlewild Church, who has read and reread, organized and reorganized, bound and rebound countless versions of the manuscript of this effort. In it all, she went far beyond efficiency and was full of good cheer and kind words. I am likewise grateful to Pat Taylor, who patiently and thoroughly proofread each draft of the manuscript. She can not only spot a misspelled word or a comma splice from across the room, she can also diagnose syntax problems and make suggestions without doing damage to the writer's ego. Many thanks also to Michael Wilt of Saint Mary's Press, who has been extraordinarily helpful throughout the project.

In much more personal ways, I wish to express my gratitude to our daughters, Jayne Lowry and Nichols Lowry. Even as adults who should know better, they continue to think I am the best preacher there is. Since it is for them true, their view represents dearly that place very near the heart of pure grace without which no one can fully live.

Above all I am grateful to Martha Nichols Lowry for more than three-and-a-half decades of devoted support despite the insanity incumbent on the profession to which I was called and despite the added tomfoolery with which I practice it. Greater love hath no one. With boundless thanks, these pages are dedicated to her.

J. S. L.
Idlewild Church
January 1999

# Introduction

The primary purpose of this book is to provide thought-provoking material for those who enjoy being reflective about the world and its people, or for those who long to be reflective about the world and its people. I am a Christian minister, which makes me comfortable in the realm of devotional material for people of the church. Indeed, members of the Christian community using the book might find it helpful for their seasonal private or group worship. Though the texts are random selections, some readers may find the book helpful as a resource for Bible study. In addition to believers, however, I want to invite those who are not part of the church community to explore with me a select collection of insights, born in Christian literature, that I believe can expand human insight and emotion beyond the traditions of the church. In all events, whether in or out of church, I sincerely hope the reader will find this material enriching and entertaining.

A secondary purpose of this book is to provide for the preachers of the church examples of sermons written by one who self-consciously claims the identity of artist. Indeed, a basic premise of this volume is that the Christian practice of preaching the Gospel of Jesus Christ is an art form wherein the preacher, as artist, presents biblical truth to a worshiping congregation. A further premise of this volume is that at their best, preachers, as artists, are the ones selected by their respective worshiping communities and given the unique responsibility of going often to Holy Scripture on behalf of a congregation. From Holy Scripture, the preacher, as artist, having used the best scholarship available in preparation, is to return to the congregation with a message from God so utterly overwhelming that it can only be contained and presented as a work of art generated from deep within the preacher's imagination. By pointing to truth far greater than itself, the work of art is expected to elicit from the congregation responses that can vary from time to time and place to place but, in the words of the great hymn, must always leave the congregation "lost in wonder, love, and praise."[1]

Not surprisingly, then, this book is composed of sermons. Several of the sermons had their genesis in other congregations, but as presented here they are taken almost verbatim from manuscripts used for morning worship at the Idlewild Presbyterian Church of Memphis, Tennessee. Idlewild is a large urban congregation of the Presbyterian Church (U.S.A.). It has a long-standing tradition of being both servant and prophet to the city. The Idlewild congregation worships in a cathedral setting.

As in other art forms, preaching will, of course, vary in style, excellence, and maturity. Moreover, because the art is preaching in the context of the Christian community, it will also vary in theological presupposition and insight. Unlike other art forms, however, in preaching, *form* can never overshadow *content*. That is, whereas a great painting or great symphony may, on occasion, exist only for the sake of its own beauty, such can never be the case for the art of preaching. In preaching, both art and artist must always be the servant of what the artist considers divine truth.

For purposes of this or any book of sermons, it must be remembered that preaching is an oral art form. Indeed, by some definitions, "published sermon" and "book of sermons" may well be oxymorons. That is, as soon as a sermon is published, it may no longer be a sermon. The question is not whether sermons should be written. The question is whether sermons should be or even can be read by anyone other than the artists who wrote them. Contrary to some popular beliefs, most faithful sermons are, at some point, committed to paper. Even those excellent preachers who enter the pulpit with few or no notes have, with almost no exceptions, spent hours and hours in preparation, planning carefully the presentation of their art down to the selection of each word. The truth to be presented in the preaching event is far too important and far too vast to be trusted, in most instances, to nothing but spontaneity. For most good preachers, the Holy Spirit moves through the preacher working long hours with pen in hand or, more recently, seated at a word processor.

Whether this or any book of sermons is used devotionally or as an example of preaching, the real issue is whether the sermons can, with theological and artistic integrity, become something to be consumed visually. The obvious answer is *yes, maybe*. There are countless examples where the transition has been made successfully. The

Bible, of course, is the best imaginable case in point. All, or virtually all, of the Bible was written with an assumption that its words would be heard. Because the books of the Bible predate the printing press by centuries, copies of the texts were scarce. Moreover, many of the people for whom the books of the Bible were written, it is safe to assume, were unable to read. Surely the writers, redactors, editors (artists!) assumed that the books would be heard. They must have written with no other alternative in mind. Indeed, that is why many observers have noted that Scripture is best understood and experienced when it is read aloud.

For quite different reasons, preachers write with the same limitations and the same opportunities as the biblical writers (and editors or redactors). That is, although printing is readily available and most people in most congregations can read, preachers, when writing, must assume that their work will be heard and not seen. For that reason, the reader of these or any sermons, although he or she cannot avoid seeing the text, is advised to read the sermons aloud if at all possible.

The sermons contained here were selected with two unifying elements in mind. The first is that most of the texts on which the sermons were written appear in *The Revised Common Lectionary*. I have included in the notes the year and day for which each text is listed. Variations are likewise noted.

The second unifying element is that all but one of the sermons contained here use narrative as a homiletical method. With only two exceptions, the stories are taken from my extended family and are strongly influenced by my family's faith commitments and tradition of storytelling. My earliest formative years were spent with my mother in or near the respective homes of my mother's parents and my father's parents. My grandparents were all gifted storytellers in the tradition of the rural Deep South, where both of my grandfathers were "gentleman farmers."

During those early years, my father was in Europe for most of World War II. Following the war and my father's return home, my two brothers and I settled with our parents on a farm in the Piedmont area of South Carolina near the small town of Great Falls. Farming was mostly a hobby for my father, but because he came from a long line of farmers, from his birth to his death farming remained an integral part of his identity and, through him, was formative for me and my preaching.

In the years following the war and until my graduation from high school in 1958, in many ways our lives focused on the Great Falls Presbyterian Church. At the Great Falls Presbyterian Church, careful attention to excellent preaching and participation in faithful Christian education could be and were assumed for all of its two hundred members. My close tie to that worshiping community is also an integral part of my preaching.

The sermons here are only slightly edited versions of the manuscripts used for morning worship at the Idlewild Church. At the beginning of my career, I developed a strange system for the placement of the sermons on the page as a means of making it easier to find and keep my place while preaching from a full manuscript and, at the same time, maintain eye contact with members of the congregation. Over the years, however, the form has taken on a life of its own and now often reflects the meter and flow of the sermons. Each sermon was originally written entirely with the lines broken and paragraph divisions inverted. For purposes here I have revised much of the purely narrative material to make it easier to read. The remainder of each sermon is left in its original form with the hope that the broken lines and inverted paragraphs will help the reader develop a sense of reading for oral interpretation. Perhaps what originated as a style to make it easier to read aloud can now make it easier for the reader to "hear" the meditations. When I write, I imagine sound. Beyond the narratives, I have not altered my style. I hope the style will help draw the reader into those sounds and the truth I long for the sounds to convey.

# Part 1
# Advent
# and
# Christmas

# Low-Back, Ladder-Back, Cane-Bottom Chair with the Legs Cut Off Just So

Rejoice in the Lord always; again I will say, Rejoice. Let your gentleness be known to everyone. The Lord is near. Do not worry about anything, but in everything by prayer and supplication with thanksgiving let your requests be made known to God. And the peace of God, which surpasses all understanding, will guard your hearts and your minds in Christ Jesus. (Philippians 4:4–7)[1]

And Mary said,
    "My soul magnifies the Lord. . . .
    He has shown strength with his arm;
        he has scattered the proud in the thoughts of their hearts.
    He has brought down the powerful from their thrones,
        and lifted up the lowly;
    he has filled the hungry with good things,
        and sent the rich away empty."

(Luke 1:46,51–53)[2]

---

What sentry is this
    who guards our hearts
    and stands guard at the threshold of our lives?
What peace have we
    to keep at bay any last enemy
    who would venture into our days?
        These are questions that must be answered
            by sermon's end.

For now I want you to know of a ladder-back cane-bottom chair that sits catercornered beside my closet. Many years ago, the Sentry

7

of God stood guard stationed beside that chair. Some mornings still, if I take time to think of it, I get the feeling that the Sentry of God is still stationed beside that chair.

It's not a high ladder-back cane-bottom chair but a short ladder-back cane-bottom chair of the sort that you find on the back porch of country houses where folks sit to talk in the summer while they shell peas or shuck corn or peel peaches.

My low-back ladder-back cane-bottom chair also has short legs. They were cut off, just so, to accommodate one Bessie Grier.

Bessie Grier was a short woman. She is the one beside whom, I choose to believe, the Sentry of God stood guard, though I must say I never thought of it in just that way until this text from Paul's letter to the Philippians grabbed hold, shook me good, and wouldn't let go until I listened carefully.

Bessie Grier kept the chair not on the back porch but in the kitchen beside the stove. A long time ago she sat in it every day to rest from her labor. Today I sit in it nearly every day to put on my socks and shoes. It's just the right height for putting on socks and shoes. If you want to know the truth, however, putting on my socks and shoes is just a good excuse to sit in that chair every day.

> Now that the Apostle Paul has given me the image,
>   I think I shall try to think every day
>   of the Sentry of God
>   standing beside that chair
>   to keep at bay any ultimate harm
>   that might otherwise come to me that day.

Bessie Grier was born some twenty years after President Abraham Lincoln signed the Emancipation Proclamation. She was never, however, completely emancipated. Progress in those days was slow as now: three steps forward, two steps backward.

At the time I came into Bessie's life, the whole world was at war with itself for the second time. When the world is at war with itself, it is not the season to correct the domestic evil of two or three hundred years' duration. So, like her parents before her who were slaves, Bessie Grier served her white folks and depended on our generosity. We were gentle and kind enough. In some ways we were ahead of our time. In other ways we knew not what we did.

You could tell from her long, graceful fingers that Bessie Grier had been born to be tall. Her feet also were too big for her four-foot-six-inch frame. Both legs were short, but one was shorter than the other. She must have had polio along the way. That's why the legs on her chair were cut short.

> I choose to believe
> > the Sentry of God once stood guard
> > beside that chair
> > every day
> > so no ultimate harm
> > could come to her.

Two dollars a week was the going wage back then for five and a half days of domestic work. Every day before sunup Bessie Grier came from her shanty up to the big house to cook breakfast for us. She stayed until supper was on the table.

She cooked dinner, too, but that was in the middle of the day back then.

Between cooking and cleaning, she put bandages on skinned white knees; she dried tears on white cheeks; and, with the gentle sway of her body, she rocked white babies in her lap. Her short-legged chair had no rockers.

All the while she sang songs of her sweet little Jesus boy, of layin' down her burden by the riverside, and of being nearer to her God.

That she loved us says more good of her character than of ours.

> I now think she was able to love us
> > because the Sentry of God
> > was standing guard beside her chair
> > and she knew no power on earth
> > could at last undo her.

And she did love us. There is freedom in loving children. I remember the times in summer when the days were long and hot and she would take us home with her after supper to play hide-and-seek in the cornfield beside her shanty. Hand in hand we'd walk—me and an assortment of my brothers and cousins—with Bessie Grier down the lane, across the highway, past the cotton gin.

The gin not only separated the cotton from the seed, it also separated the white folks and the black folks . . . at night.

Each trip home with Bessie Grier ended with a treat . . . a treat of great, great value . . . like the magic she spun with bright yellow lemons, of which she seldom had more than one at any time. As though the lemon were purest gold, with children gathered round, she would hold it in her long, graceful fingers and caress its waxy skin so that eagerness mounted among us as she chuckled almost silently.

Then, with great ceremony, she made lemonade for everybody and everybody laughed, even though there was no joke.

Lemonade made with a lemon of great value
    to be shared in love
    is the best lemonade there is.
Laughing with those whom you love
    when there is no joke
    is the best laughter there is.
I know now
    she was able to love
    and to laugh
    because she knew the Sentry of God
    stood by her chair
    so that no ultimate harm
    would come to her.
Aren't you glad Paul gave us that image!
    He dropped it right there
        out of nowhere
        except his great heart
        and he put that image
        right in the middle of his letter
        to the Philippians . . .
        at least it's in the middle as we now have it.
    Out of place, some would say.
    It's a benediction . . . a blessing . . .
        in the middle of his letter.
    In the form of the day
        a blessing like that
        is supposed to be at the end of the letter.

Maybe the letter ended there once
    and he added a P. S.
Who knows?
It's in the middle now
    and he didn't move the blessing
    if he had an after-blessing thought.

Do you get the picture?
Paul was writing his dear, dear friends.
Paul groused a bit
    in his letter to the Ephesians
    and he groused a lot
    in his letters to the Corinthians.
They weren't doing everything just right
    and Paul told them so . . .
    in no uncertain terms.

But the letter to the Philippians?
The letter to the Philippians
    is a love letter
    pure and simple
    from Paul to the church.

In the middle of the letter,
    so out of place
    it couldn't be there by mistake,
    is a benediction . . . a blessing.
You get the feeling
    it just overflowed into the text.
In that blessing is this wonderful image:
    "The peace of God is standing guard."

Listen to more of the blessing:
    "Rejoice in the Lord,"
        the blessing begins.
    "Let everyone know of your forbearance. . . ."
        and then,
    "The peace of God is standing guard
        in Christ Jesus our Lord."[3]

With the peace of God standing guard, Bessie Grier sang of her sweet little Jesus boy . . . she sang of layin' down her burden . . . she sang of being nearer to her God.

I remember especially the Christmas of the broom straw. I'm sure my brothers and cousins remember it as well. No one can remember whether it was the Christmas of the tricycle, or the Christmas of the bicycle, or the Christmas of the electric train. Memories of bicycles and electric trains lie forgotten with the rest or melt into one; but the children, all now long since adults, remember in finest detail the Christmas of the broom straw. We remember as though it happens now.

We remember the knock at the back door of the big house in the dark of the night before Christmas. There she stood, Bessie Grier, huddled against the cold in her secondhand coat, too long by a foot, laughing all over without making a sound.

She held out toy brooms, as though they were more precious than myrrh—one each for me and my brothers and cousins. The brooms were made of field straw neatly tied together with bits of scrap string.

How cold and scared she must have been to walk at night past the gin. I understand now that only a person who knows the Sentry of God standing guard could have possibly dared to walk past the gin in the dark of night to deliver the gifts that would bring a hush to the big house.

In the story of our faith
    when Mary who was to become the mother of Jesus
    found out she was expecting a baby
    she wrote a poem.
        Part of the poem goes like this:

*My soul magnifies the Lord. . . .*
*For the Lord has regarded*
        *the low estate of his handmaiden.*
*The Lord has scattered the proud. . . .*
*He has put down the mighty. . . .*
*And exalted those of low degree.*

There is, of course,
　　neither value nor virtue in being poor.
There is no honor
　　in keeping others poor.
And there is romance neither in slavery
　　nor in its aftermath.

　　　It is true, however,
　　　　　when God chose to become a person
　　　　　God chose to be born
　　　　　among the have-nots;
　　　　　and when God chose to become flesh
　　　　　God chose to join the dispossessed;
　　　　　and when God chose to lay his head
　　　　　with the likes of us
　　　　　God made a bed
　　　　　with those who knew no freedom
　　　　　save the freedom
　　　　　that comes from knowing love
　　　　　and from knowing in love
　　　　　that no ultimate harm can come.

What, then, are we to say?
Is it wrong to have been born,
　　as I was,
　　　with a silver spoon in one's mouth?
Is it wrong by hard work
　　to make a comfortable life for one's self
　　and one's family?
Has God some prejudice against
　　the likes of most of us?
Is our pain less real?
Is our need less great?
**No!**
It's just that the likes of us
　　have to listen more carefully
　　to hear the angels singing.
We have many gods vying to save us
　　when we know there is, in truth,
　　but one God who can save.

For us, it's like it is
>   in the famous children's story *The Little Prince.*
In that story,
>   you may remember,
>   the little prince finds great joy
>   in caring for one rose;
>   but, when in his travels,
>   he comes across a garden with five thousand roses
>   he becomes very sad.[4]
In the face of so many roses
>   it's hard to see the beauty of one single rose.
With so many hopes fulfilled
>   we must listen more carefully than many
>   for the presence and the coming
>   of the one true hope.

Once many years after the Christmas-in-broom-straw, when I was an up-and-coming young preacher, Martha and I took our first-born home to show her off at Christmas. Bessie Grier waited for just the right moment and caught me alone in the kitchen. She put a steaming hot candied apple in a saucer on the table in front of me and motioned for me to sit and eat. She didn't have to motion but once.

She sat beside the stove in her low-back ladder-back cane-bottom chair with the legs cut off just so. Looking me square in the eye she said, "They tell me you're a full preacher now. I'm proud."

"Thank you," I said.

"You'll say the words at my funeral." It was more a statement than a question.

I laughed and said, "Yes ma'am, if I outlive you, I'll surely be there."

She didn't laugh. Nor did she divert her gaze from my eyes. She just kept smiling. The silence was palpable.

After a while I said, "I'll be there to say the words."

"Good," she said. "Now go get me that new baby of yours so I can rock her while I sit here by the stove."

"Sweet little Jesus boy," she sang. "Born in a manger . . . we didn't know who you was."

I'm not sure now exactly how many years later it was that I kept the date I made with Bessie Grier. I do know she was almost a hundred years old when she died. I was honored to say the words of her faith over her body stretched out as it was in a rented coffin. The choir sang "Nearer, My God, to Thee."

Last year when we closed my mother's home, I brought with me Bessie Grier's low-back ladder-back cane-bottom chair . . . the one with the legs cut off just so . . . the one where the peace of God stood as a Sentry keeping guard over Bessie Grier. (I'm glad Paul gave us that image.) As I said, I keep Bessie Grier's chair sitting cater-cornered by my closet. I sit in it every morning to put on my socks and shoes. Some mornings, when I have my head screwed on and my heart in gear, meaning I'm not in too big a hurry, I think of sweet little Jesus boy and of laying down my burdens and of being near to my God.

> On those days I know especially
> that the Sentry of God is keeping guard still
> and that in Christ Jesus
> there will be no injustice so great
> that it cannot be faced with dignity;
> and I know in Christ Jesus
> there will be no evil so cruel
> that it cannot be put to shame with kindness;
> and I know in Christ Jesus
> there is no grief so deep
> that it cannot be soothed with love;
> and at last I know in Christ Jesus
> there is no power so profane
> that it will not be defeated.

Idlewild Church
Third Sunday in Advent, 1994

# Mary's Song

In those days Mary set out and went with haste to a Judean town in the hill country, where she entered the house of Zechariah and greeted Elizabeth. When Elizabeth heard Mary's greeting, the child leaped in her womb. And Elizabeth was filled with the Holy Spirit and exclaimed with a loud cry, "Blessed are you among women, and blessed is the fruit of your womb. And why has this happened to me, that the mother of my Lord comes to me? For as soon as I heard the sound of your greeting, the child in my womb leaped for joy. And blessed is she who believed that there would be a fulfillment of what was spoken to her by the Lord."

And Mary said,

"My soul magnifies the Lord,
    and my spirit rejoices in God my Savior,
for he has looked with favor on the lowliness of his servant.
    Surely, from now on all generations will call me blessed;
for the Mighty One has done great things for me,
    and holy is his name.
His mercy is for those who fear him
    from generation to generation.
He has shown strength with his arm;
    he has scattered the proud in the thoughts of their hearts.
He has brought down the powerful from their thrones,
    and lifted up the lowly;
he has filled the hungry with good things,
    and sent the rich away empty.
He has helped his servant Israel,
    in remembrance of his mercy,
according to the promise he made to his ancestors,
    to Abraham and to his descendants forever."

And Mary remained with her about three months and then returned to her home. (Luke 1:39–56)[1]

---

We're about to stand on holy ground, you know,
    and we have to get ready.
We can't just let it happen,
    though, of course,
    Christmas will happen whether we are ready or not.
It's an important thing we're about to do . . .
    important and holy . . .
    far more important than shopping
    and much more holy.
We can't just let something so important
    and so uncommonly holy
    just happen.
        Soon we shall pause once more
            in time
            and wrap ourselves
            in the mantle of eternity remembered.
        On Christmas Eve,
            while standing at a particular place,
            we shall gaze once more
            into the flesh of our finite fingers
            as we close them gently about a candle . . .
            a candle held in memory
            of infinity once visited.
        From that posture of memory
            we shall wait . . .
            we shall wait with certainty . . .
            certainty of that other moment
            when time shall at last meet eternity once more;
            and when the finite shall at last meet infinity again.
        For such an event as shall happen on Christmas Eve
            we cannot be unprepared.
        We must make a careful plan.

Two women once made plans for Christmas.
Cousins.
One too old,
    most would say,
    to be expecting a baby.

The other too young,
    some would say,
    to be expecting a baby.
Girl talk is what they were about.

Girl talk, indeed!
It was unlike any girl talk I ever imagined;
    but then,
    my imagination in matters of girl talk
    is born of generations of too much prejudice.

They weren't girls at all.
They were women.
W-O-M-E-N . . .
    women . . .
    women
    into whose lives the hope of the world had been entrusted.

According to the tradition of the church,
    their woman talk went like this:

> "Blessed are you among women,"
>     said the older to the younger.
> "When I heard your voice
>     the baby leaped in my womb."

>     As every mother knows,
>         and as everyone else must surely learn,
>         it is God who inspires
>         the leaping of unborn children.
>     At the moment of first movement,
>         I am given to understand,
>         there is no doubt among women
>         that the sovereign will of God is unfolding.[2]

> "My soul magnifies the Lord,
>     and my spirit rejoices in God my Savior,"
>     replied the younger to the older.

Not like any girl talk I ever imagined;
    but then, as I said before,
    because of my gender
    my imagination in such matters
    is clearly lacking luster.
        The sovereign will of God
           was unfolding in their lives.
    They had to make ready.

We have to get ready too, you know.
We can't just let Christmas happen,
    though, of course,
    Christmas will happen whether we are ready or not.

My Grandmother Lowry made quite a to-do of getting ready for Christmas. I remember going once with her to deliver a fruitcake to one of her well-to-do friends. It was in Seneca, South Carolina, where she lived and raised her children: the Up Country they called it.

I got to go because I had helped to bake the cake. It had been my job to chop the nuts and cut the candied fruit into small pieces . . . a task I had to be convinced was suitable for a man-child.

As I cut and she mixed, she half hummed and half sang in her clear alto voice,

        "Gentle Mary laid her child
          Lowly in a manger."

That was not girl talk I now know.
At least it was not idle chatter.
It was a remarkable lesson
    to be learned from a remarkable woman
    well versed in the pain
    and joy
    and wisdom
    that come from childbirth.

Anyway, when we delivered the cake to her well-to-do friend, we were, of course, invited into the parlor. It was quite formal and quite fine. As previously instructed, I sat quietly and only spoke when spoken to . . . a lesson I have since forgotten.

From the corner of my eye, however, I could see on a table across the room the most magnificent manger scene I had yet or have yet seen. No doubt seeing me glance in its direction, and at last, taking me by the hand to be sure I wouldn't touch, our hostess invited me to walk with her to look more closely.

As we looked, my grandmother took my other hand as a double measure of insurance and explained that all the figures were made of finest china . . . so fine, in fact, that our hostess had not trusted the pieces to be packaged for shipment but had wrapped them in tissue and held them in her lap for the long trip across the Atlantic Ocean, all the way from England where they had been made.

They were all in purest white. You could almost see through the angels' wings. The shepherd's crook was as fine as a thread. The swaddling clothes were paper thin and gave the appearance of wondrous softness. Mary's hands and fingers were clearly defined and nothing so much as fragile except gentle more even than fragile.

"Gentle Mary laid her child . . ."

The lesson I learned
    was that something holy was happening . . .
    something so holy and precious it could not be touched.

      That's a wonderful lesson to learn from two women
        both of whom were well versed
        in standing reverently
        before that which is unspeakably holy.

          The unfolding of the sovereign will of God
          is always unspeakably holy.
          It cannot be touched.

In the story of getting ready for the birth of Jesus,
    the older woman was named Elizabeth.
        The name of her baby was to be John . . .
        John the Baptizer.
In the story,
    the younger woman was named Mary.
        The name of her baby was to be Jesus.

From the very beginning the church
    remembered the story of Jesus
    and the church told it by word of mouth
    from generation to generation.

At last, however,
    it became important for the church to write the story
    so that it would never be forgotten by any generation.
Several people wrote the story of Jesus.
You know them:
    Matthew, Mark, Luke, John . . .
    maybe others
    but those four are the ones saved by our tradition.

Of the four that we saved,
    only two tell the story of the birth of Jesus:
    Matthew and Luke.
Of the two,
    Luke is the only one who remembered to save for us
    the remarkable story
    of two remarkable women getting ready for Christmas.

        The older woman said to the younger,
          *"Blessed are you, Mary,*
            *because you believed*
            *there would be a fulfillment in you*
            *of what God promised the world God would do."*
    And according to the story as it has been saved for us,
        the younger woman sang to the older,
          *"God has exalted those of low degree*
            *and scattered the proud*
            *in the imagination of their hearts."*
            By the time Luke wrote the story
              the proud had already been
                scattered.
          Like now,
            the proud in the state;
            the proud of the market; and
            the proud in the church
               had no reason left to be proud.
              More about that later.

This is a story about getting ready for Christmas.
We have to get ready, don't we.
We can't just let Christmas happen,
    though, of course,
    the sovereign will of God *shall* unfold
    whether we are ready or not.

My Grandmother Banks made quite a to-do of getting ready for Christmas, too; but getting ready for Christmas at my Grandmother Banks's house was a lot different than getting ready for Christmas at my Grandmother Lowry's house.

My Grandmother Banks lived in Saint Matthews, South Carolina: the Low Country they call it. Both of my grandmothers baked fruitcakes, and like Tom Sawyer, they managed to convince their various grandchildren that chopping nuts and cutting up candied fruit was a task of great honor.

Other than that, almost nothing was the same about my grandmothers. Their fruitcakes didn't even smell alike. As it happened, my Grandmother Banks had a secret ingredient she poured over the top of the fruitcake after the cake had had a chance to cool. She got the special ingredient from Kentucky where, she explained, they are especially gifted at making it. She further explained the secret ingredient was to keep the cake moist, but while she poured the secret ingredient she sang,

           "'Tis the season to be jolly."

Not a bad lesson to be learned . . .
I mean the being jolly part.

The crèche at my Grandmother Banks's house was different, too . . . not much at all like the lovely delicate one in the parlor of my Grandmother Lowry's friend. My Grandmother Banks's crèche was built with children in mind. She had a great gourd almost as big as a bushel basket. My Grandfather Banks had cut a hole in the side of the gourd and painted the inside dark blue to look like the sky. He dotted the sky with stars and then he did a most remarkable thing. He installed a little electric light in the sky that could be turned on to be the Christmas star.

Best of all, they had a shoebox filled to overflowing with a wonderful assortment of mix-and-match figures. Most of the figures
were chipped and bruised, and the angels' wings were bent from
years of touching and pretending. For weeks before Christmas, as a
way of getting ready, the gourd was kept on the floor with the box of
figures beside it. Together they were an invitation for children of all
ages to arrange and rearrange the figures and to tell the story to anyone who would listen; and, of course, most important of all, it was a
chance for little people and big people alike to become part of the
story of that remarkable birth.

Touching the story
        and believing yourself to be part of the story
        are most remarkable lessons
        to be learned from a most remarkable woman
        who herself knew well
        the pain and
        the joy and
        the hope
        that come with giving birth.

What is this thing we do at Christmas?
Is it something so holy it cannot be touched;
        we can only stand quietly and pray?
Is it something so human it has to be touched and held
        lest it get away?

            It is, of course,
                both of those.

Here at the heart of what we do on Christmas Eve
        we are able to stand in time
        and wrap ourselves
        in the mantle of eternity remembered.
Here with these finite fingers
        we are allowed for a moment
        to touch the memory of infinity.
            It happened then
                in the birthing of a baby.

It happens now
in the rebirthing of something in us.
It is the hope we have
in the unfolding
of the sovereign will of God.

We'll let the experts
worry about whether Mary really wrote this poem or not.
Some folks think maybe
it's a hymn the church sang early on
when they told the story of Elizabeth and Mary.
Either way it's a nice thought.
We call it the Magnificat:

"My soul magnifies the Lord,"
she sang
and the church after her.
It's the way she felt
and the way we feel
at the hope of Christmas
being fulfilled in her
and in us.

As I said earlier,
for generations
the story was passed by word of mouth
and the church sang Mary's Song.
By the time Luke wrote it to save it forever
the world he knew had collapsed.
Quite literally,
Luke's world offered no hope.
The best effort of Caesar Augustus
to force the world to live at peace
had failed miserably.
For practical purposes
there was no government to provide order;
there was no market to provide goods . . .
and there was no temple to provide God.
Everything was in shambles.

Like now
    when it is obvious on all sides
    that the anger and frustration we face
    are too complex for government to salve;
    and the deficit is so large
    our children may drown in our excesses;
    and all the while the denominations
    are tearing themselves apart
    while the world yawns
    in the face of the church.

But hear this:
It was against just such a background
    that Luke wrote his story of Jesus.
And against that hopeless setting,
    unlike the others,
    Luke chose to begin his Gospel account
    with this remarkable story
    of these remarkable women
    so filled with hope
    as they got ready for Christmas . . .
    filled with hope
    as they got ready for the sovereign will of God
    to unfold in their lives.

That's the story the church must tell.
No matter what's going on in our world,
    that's the story the church must live
    and that's the story about which the church must sing.

As to the whereabouts of the crèche of my Grandmother Lowry's friend, I can only speculate. It's so lovely I have to believe it is somewhere working its magic and telling its story of something so unspeakably holy it cannot be touched.

As to the whereabouts of my Grandmother Banks's crèche, there was a fire in our family home, and along with everything else the crèche was burned. But, unknown to any of us, every fall for a number of years, my father, a great grower of gourds, began saving the seeds from the largest gourd of summer. Every spring he planted the seeds; and every fall he saved the seeds from the largest gourd. It was during those years when his sons were distracted with college and graduate school and getting married.

Before too many years, though, Pappy had nurtured the growth of a gourd large enough to be set aside for its holy but altogether touchable purpose. Where my mother found the hodgepodge of figures, I haven't the slightest idea, but there they were on the floor at Christmas just in time for our children and their cousins to touch and pretend and learn.

The gourd now waits for yet another generation. Who knows, perhaps more than all others they will need to touch the story as they prepare for the sovereign will of God to unfold in yet another generation living in the need of hope.

Idlewild Church
Fourth Sunday in Advent, 1992

# Listening for the Christmas Angel

An account of the genealogy of Jesus the Messiah, the son of David, the son of Abraham.

Abraham was the father of Isaac, and Isaac the father of Jacob, and Jacob the father of Judah and his brothers, and Judah the father of Perez and Zerah by Tamar, and Perez the father of Hezron, and Hezron the father of Aram, and Aram the father of Aminadab, and Aminadab the father of Nahshon, and Nahshon the father of Salmon, and Salmon the father of Boaz by Rahab, and Boaz the father of Obed by Ruth, and Obed the father of Jesse, and Jesse the father of King David.

And David was the father of Solomon by the wife of Uriah, and Solomon the father of Rehoboam, and Rehoboam the father of Abijah, and Abijah the father of Asaph, and Asaph the father of Jehoshaphat, and Jehoshaphat the father of Joram, and Joram the father of Uzziah, and Uzziah the father of Jotham, and Jotham the father of Ahaz, and Ahaz the father of Hezekiah, and Hezekiah the father of Manasseh, and Manasseh the father of Amos, and Amos the father of Josiah, and Josiah the father of Jechoniah and his brothers, at the time of the deportation to Babylon.

And after the deportation to Babylon: Jechoniah was the father of Salathiel, and Salathiel the father of Zerubbabel, and Zerubbabel the father of Abiud, and Abiud the father of Eliakim, and Eliakim the father of Azor, and Azor the father of Zadok, and Zadok the father of Achim, and Achim the father of Eliud, and Eliud the father of Eleazar, and Eleazar the father of Matthan, and Matthan the father of Jacob, and Jacob the father of Joseph the husband of Mary, of whom Jesus was born, who is called the Messiah.

So all the generations from Abraham to David are fourteen generations; and from David to the deportation to Babylon, fourteen generations; and from the deportation to Babylon to the Messiah, fourteen generations.

Now the birth of Jesus the Messiah took place in this way. When his mother Mary had been engaged to Joseph, but before they lived together, she was found to be with child from the Holy Spirit. Her husband Joseph, being a righteous man and unwilling to expose her to public disgrace, planned to dismiss her quietly. But just when he had resolved to do this, an angel of the Lord appeared to him in a dream and said, "Joseph, son of David, do not be afraid to take Mary as your wife, for the child conceived in her is from the Holy Spirit. She will bear a son, and you are to name him Jesus, for he will save his people from their sins." All this took place to fulfill what had been spoken by the Lord through the prophet:

"Look, the virgin shall conceive and bear a son,
and they shall name him Emmanuel,"

which means, "God is with us." When Joseph awoke from sleep, he did as the angel of the Lord commanded him; he took her as his wife, but had no marital relations with her until she had borne a son; and he named him Jesus. (Matthew 1:1–25)[1]

———————

Listen!
Listen ever so carefully.
Listen to see if you can hear the Christmas angel singing.

Can you hear?
Sometimes I think I can.
In fact,
    I think I heard the Christmas angel only a few weeks ago.

Just so you will know
    what you hear
    when you hear the Christmas angel singing
    is really
    the Christmas angel singing,
    let me give you the lyrics
    to the Christmas angel song . . .

not the Christmas angel as Luke told it . . .
everybody knows that Christmas angel song:

*Glory to God in the highest*
*and on earth peace!*

It's a beautiful song;
>but this morning I want to give you
>the lyrics of the Christmas angel song
>>as Matthew remembered them
>>and passed them along. . . .

>Are you ready? . . .

>Here goes:
>>*Don't be afraid.*
>>*The baby is from God.*
>>*Name him Jesus.*
>>*He will save his people* . . .
>>*save them from their sins.*
>>*Name him.*
>>*Claim him.*
>>*Claim him as your own.*

I wonder if the President will be able to hear
>the Christmas angel singing this year?

>>I hope so.
>>I earnestly hope so.

I wonder if the members of Congress will be able to hear
>the Christmas angel singing this year?

>>I hope so.
>>I earnestly hope so.

I wonder if the people of this once proud nation will be able to hear
>the Christmas angel singing this year?

>>I hope so.
>>I earnestly hope so.

This much is clear:

> *If you want to hear the Christmas angel sing,*
> *it's not enough*
> *merely*
> *to do the right thing.*
> *If you want to hear the Christmas angel sing,*
> *indisputably*
> *right motive*
> *is the necessary thing.*

The Christmas angel will, of course,
    sing to whomever the Christmas angel wishes.
        It's the way of messengers from God.
        God's messengers do as God chooses.

        Still,
            if the story of Joseph is to be trusted,
            a good way to put yourself in a posture
            for hearing the Christmas angel

            when the Christmas angel sings
            is to make it a practice,
            in all matters,
            to do the right thing
            for exactly
            the right reason;

            and, after all,
            Christmas is an excellent time
            to get into the practice
            of doing the right thing
            for exactly the right reason.

As I said, I think I heard the Christmas angel singing not so very long ago . . . back at Thanksgiving it was. I hadn't at all planned to hear the Christmas angel singing that early; but, now that I think about it, I'm sure it's what I heard.

It happened like this. Both of my brothers and their whole families came to visit us in Memphis for Thanksgiving. Came on Wednesday. Stayed till Sunday. It was a grand weekend. We had a wonderful time . . . a weekend truly filled with wonder.

Now, in order for you to know exactly how I came to hear the Christmas angel singing at Thanksgiving, I must tell you that until very recently our daughters and all their cousins were old enough that none of them would want me to tell you their ages. Then my brother Banks and his wife, Mary Willa, brought Eliza into our family . . . a miracle baby by any way of judging miracles. Eliza is four now; and all of a sudden, there is another little person at the table; and what joy she has brought!

In honor of the occasion of Eliza's first visit to our house, Eliza's Uncle Jim, that's me, when out to his shop and built her a music box . . . a beautiful thing if I do say so myself . . . built out of fine walnut . . . with a little compartment where treasures can be stored.

Would you believe the music box plays three tunes! When Uncle Jim, that's me, got ready to order the music works, Uncle Jim couldn't make up his mind among "Thank Heaven for Little Girls," "It's a Small World After All," and "Somewhere Over the Rainbow," so crazy Uncle Jim, that's me, ordered all three thinking he would make up his mind later.

In the end, he decided to install all three. No family is complete without one crazy uncle; but this crazy Uncle Jim, for all of his craziness, got to hear the Christmas angel sing.

The angel didn't sing to the melody of the music box playing. Oh no. In fact, when Eliza wound all three tunes at the same time it was nothing so much as a cacophony; but, those with ears to hear could hear the Christmas angel singing in Eliza's innocent and genuine delight and see the Christmas angel reflected in the mist of her parents' eyes. Crazy Uncle Jim did the right thing; and, at least for once, he did it for the right reason: Welcome to the family, Eliza. Welcome to the table.

Oh, I know.
I know.
I know well.
I know full well.
Doing the right thing for the right reason
    is not always that easy;

    but it is always that important.

The President
    has again
    sent our young men and young women to war . . .
    lasted only four days this time.
        No one can be sure
            his motives were pure.
        Nor can anyone be sure
            his motives were impure.

The chambers of Congress,
    each in its turn,
    are doing their part
    to place the President on trial
    for high crimes and misdemeanors.
        No one can be sure
            their motives are pure.
        Nor can anyone be sure
            their motives are impure.

            The nation is in crisis.
            We the people must now
                add grief to our embarrassment.
            Never in my memory
                has motive ever mattered more.

Some of my preacher friends are a lot more sure than I
    that they know the correct course of action
    for the body politic.[2]

I see no clear direction for the church to advise.
Only of this
    am I absolutely sure:

        This year,
            in the telling of the story of the birth of our Lord,
            by some twist of sure providence,
            the Joseph text is the recommended point of departure
            for the church to take on this,
            the Sunday before Christmas

which is, by chance,
the Sunday after war
and the Sunday between impeachment and trial.

> The Joseph text,
>> I suspect,
>>> is no one's favorite.
>>>> Joseph, after all,
>>>>> by some ways of thinking,
>>>>>> is not even a major player in the drama.
>>>> He's not the "real" father of Jesus.

My friend John Buchanan, pastor of Fourth Presbyterian Church of Chicago, tells about a four-year-old girl named Megan, a friend's niece, who drew a picture of the nativity. When she completed the work, she explained each of the characters to her mother: shepherds and sheep, three wise men and camels, the stable with cows and a cat and dog and the manger and, of course, Mary and the baby.

"Where's Joseph?" asked Megan's mom.

"Who needs Joseph?" replied Megan.

Megan is, no doubt, a feminist theologian in the making.[3]

Well, Megan,
> today . . .
> especially today,
> we all need Joseph.
>> We need Joseph
>>> because he not only did the right thing,
>>> he did it for the right reason.[4]

>> It's true, of course,
>>> Joseph was not Jesus' biological father.
>>> Matthew and Luke make that abundantly clear.
>> Joseph did, however,
>>> according to Matthew,
>>> give Jesus a name;
>>> and when Joseph gave Jesus a name
>>> Joseph became Jesus' daddy
>>> and that was the legal law.[5]

By giving him a name,
    Joseph assumed the right and responsibility
    to burp Jesus,
    and bounce Jesus on his knee,
    and hold Jesus close in his strong arms;
    and later to teach Jesus how to be a carpenter.
As I said,
    it was the legal law;

    but more than the legal law,
    it was through Joseph
    that Jesus was kin to the likes of Abraham,
    Ruth,
    David,
    Bathsheba.
        Certain of the promises of God
           were kept through Mary:
               *Behold a virgin shall conceive.*
        Other promises of God
           were kept through the lineage of Joseph.
        The plan of salvation from the beginning
           was passed by God to Jesus
           through the family of Joseph
           and when Joseph named the baby
           the promises were fulfilled.

Perhaps you remember having heard of the marriage customs of that time and place: With the bride no younger than twelve and the groom no younger than thirteen, a marriage was arranged by the parents of the bride and groom. After no less than a year from the time of betrothal, the groom would take his bride home where the marriage would be consummated. It was during the intervening year, between betrothal and consummation, that a rumor of scandal raised its ugly head. Mary was found to be with child. Joseph was not the father. We readers from the church knew all along what was going on; but Joseph didn't know. The baby was of the Holy Spirit. The presumption was that Mary was guilty of a capital offense. Death by stoning would have been the sure sentence.

That Joseph knew to divorce her
    means he knew to do the right thing.
    It was what the law required.
That he resolved to divorce her quietly,
    as the text says,
    means his motive was pure.

    It was a hard choice;

        but the choice was surrounded in grace.

One cannot say, of course, that the purity of Joseph's motive is what prompted the Christmas angel to sing; nor, for that matter, can we even say the purity of his motive made it possible for Joseph to hear when the angel was singing.

What we know
    is that his motive was full of grace
    and that he,
    in fact,
    heard a message from God;
    and I choose to believe the two are connected.

    "The baby is of the Holy Spirit,"
        sang the angel.
    "Claim him as your own."
    "Name the baby," sang the angel.
    "Name him Jesus . . .
        he will save his people
        from their sins."
    It's what the name happens to mean.

I wonder if the President will be able to hear
    the Christmas angel singing this year?

    I hope so.
    I earnestly hope so.

I wonder if the members of Congress will be able to hear
    the Christmas angel singing this year?
        I hope so.
        I earnestly hope so.

I wonder if the people of this once proud nation will be able to hear
    the Christmas angel singing this year?

        I no longer hope it.
        I am now sure of it.
        Many will hear.
        The ones whose choices are surrounded in grace
            will surely hear the Christmas angel.

Maybe it is not for the church to try to tell the President
    or the Congress
  what they must or must not do.

        Perhaps it is for the church
            to model for them
            the proper posture
            for listening
            for a message of hope from God.

        This much is clear:
        The Christmas angel is about to sing.
        The song will be of a child  . . .
            a little child  . . .
            a child in whose face
            is the only hope
            in which this world,
            grown crusty,
            can at last depend.

            Name him.
            Claim him.
            Claim him as your own.

        Surely he will save us from our sins.

                Idlewild Church
            Fourth Sunday in Advent, 1998

# Part 2
# Lent
# and
# Easter

# Like the Serpent in the Wilderness

From Mount Hor they set out by the way to the Red Sea, to go around the land of Edom; but the people became impatient on the way. The people spoke against God and against Moses, "Why have you brought us up out of Egypt to die in the wilderness? For there is no food and no water, and we detest this miserable food." Then the LORD sent poisonous serpents among the people, and they bit the people, so that many Israelites died. The people came to Moses and said, "We have sinned by speaking against the LORD and against you; pray to the LORD to take away the serpents from us." So Moses prayed for the people. And the LORD said to Moses, "Make a poisonous serpent, and set it on a pole; and everyone who is bitten shall look at it and live." So Moses made a serpent of bronze, and put it upon a pole; and whenever a serpent bit someone, that person would look at the serpent of bronze and live.

The Israelites set out, and camped in Oboth. (Numbers 21:4–10)[1]

Now there was a Pharisee named Nicodemus, a leader of the Jews. He came to Jesus by night and said to him, "Rabbi, we know that you are a teacher who has come from God; for no one can do these signs that you do apart from the presence of God." Jesus answered him, "Very truly, I tell you, no one can see the kingdom of God without being born from above." Nicodemus said to him, "How can anyone be born after having grown old? Can one enter a second time into the mother's womb and be born?" Jesus answered, "Very truly, I tell you, no one can enter the kingdom of God without being born of water and Spirit. What is born of the flesh is flesh, and what is born of the Spirit is spirit." . . . Nicodemus said to him, "How can these things be?" Jesus answered him, "Are you a teacher of Israel, and yet you do not understand these things?

". . . Just as Moses lifted up the serpent in the wilderness, so must the Son of Man be lifted up, that whoever believes in him may have eternal life.

"For God so loved the world that he gave his only Son, so that everyone who believes in him may not perish but may have eternal life.

"Indeed, God did not send the Son into the world to condemn the world, but in order that the world might be saved through him." (John 3:1–17)[2]

---

We buried Tex Malone so far out in the country that the grave diggers wouldn't even go out there and dig the grave. Nothing the funeral director could say or do would change their minds. They said it was just too far to move their equipment. They were probably right, especially in Alabama on a hot day in July. That it was Saturday didn't help much, I suspect.

We're going to be talking about John 3:16 today.
It's probably the most familiar verse in the Christian Bible  . . .
    too familiar some would say
    though I personally doubt if that is possible.
John 3:16 has been called the Gospel in miniature
    and it's an apt description.
        You know it well:

> For God so loved the world,
>     that he gave his only begotten Son,
>     that whosoever believeth in him
>     should not perish,
>     but have everlasting life.

That's the familiar King James Version.
Who's to argue in any version.
Preaching on John 3:16 reminds me of a speech about which I heard.
The speech was given by a famous preacher
    to some not-so-famous preachers.
        The famous preacher said
            that the annual Thanksgiving sermon
            is the most difficult sermon of the year.
                There's not much with which to disagree.

                "The preacher begins, 'Brothers and sisters,
                    we ought to be more thankful.'

There is a dramatic pause.
The preacher continues, 'I say, brothers and sisters,
    we ought to be more thankful.'

'Alright,' said the famous preacher
    to his not-so-famous colleagues,
    'you've filled thirty seconds
    but you have nineteen minutes and
    thirty seconds left.
There's no tension.
There's no mystery.'"[3]

I would not have us be one iota less familiar with John 3:16;
    but I do hope our familiarity with it has not robbed from us
    the mystery and tension of the famous text.
        That's why I want to tell you about Tex Malone.
        Tex was full of mystery and tension.

Tex's widow and their three children rode with me to the funeral: two boys and a girl rode in the backseat . . . school-age children . . . not yet in high school . . . dressed in clothes passed down to them from children in the church. Tex knew the church would see to the children no matter what.

Tex's widow rode in the front seat beside me. Her name was Marj. She was dressed in clothes passed on to her by some women in the church. She was holding Tex's Bible tight to her breast . . . the Bible they had given him in Sunday School.

We were the only car following the hearse. It was an old hearse—the one they mostly use to drive late at night to the back door of the hospital. Not the one they mostly keep polished to leave from the front door of the funeral home.

It was an old Buick, as I recall. It blew puffs of dark gray smoke from the tailpipe. I was driving my new Ford Maverick. It was the first new car I bought after I got a real job. You could buy Ford Mavericks in a variety of colors, each given names taken from the season. One possibility, for example, was anti-establish mint. That's *m-i-n-t.* It was dark green. Another possibility was Freudian gilt. That's *g-i-l-t.* It was a dusty gold color. Calvinist that I am supposed to be, I decided Freudian gilt would present a better image to the congregation than anti-establish mint.

Tex's widow and their children and I followed the smoking hearse so far out in the country we drove five miles or more past the blacktop on a gravel road. Finally we pulled into the yard of a church. The church had long since been abandoned. The windows were out. The front porch had fallen away. The sagging roof made the stub of a steeple tilt just so; but there was still a wooden cross on top of the stubby steeple.

The run-down, overgrown cemetery was in the side yard.

Two or three pickup trucks along with a rattletrap car or two were angled up to a big oak tree like spokes on a wheel so as to take advantage of the tree's shade from every angle. A half-dozen men and half as many women were leaned against the trucks talking. The men in one group and the women in another. The men were smoking and drinking. When we pulled up beside them, they went to the trucks to stash their bottles of cheap bourbon not-so-discretely covered in brown paper sacks.

One of the problems with John 3:16 being so familiar is that
    because it is so quotable on its own,
      we almost always quote it out of its context.
        I'm not going to grouse about that.
        The verse is such a jewel of wisdom and truth
          standing on its own
            that it's easy just to let it stand on its own.
        It's in its context, however, that the jewel shines brightest.

It's part of the Nicodemus story.
Presbyterians and other mainline Protestants,
    and Catholics as well, I suspect,
      don't dwell much of late on the Nicodemus story.
The Nicodemus story is one of those stories that has been so abused
    it's become almost an embarrassment to us.
Nicodemus is the one who came to Jesus in the dark of night
    because he was impressed that Jesus could turn water into wine.
      Right off
          Jesus told Nicodemus that he had to be born again . . .
          or *born from above*
          as Presbyterians and others prefer to translate it.

That's the rub.
Some highly publicized and well-intentioned people
    have defined being born again in such narrow terms
    that the rest of us have tended to shy away from it.
        That's too bad.
The Nicodemus story is so typical of John.
John is the one more than all the others,
    you may remember,
    who just loves to use irony as a literary device . . .
    literary and theological.

        When Jesus talks about being born again,
            right off Nicodemus thinks Jesus is talking
            about obstetrics and gynecology
            when Jesus and John and we, the readers,
            know Jesus is talking about something
            far more important than obstetrics and gynecology.

That also, I suppose,
    is where the rub comes.
        Being born again or born from above
            is not confined to one set of
            ecstatic religious experience.
        Being born from above is seeing truth from a whole new
            and radically different perspective . . .
            a perspective that can only be inspired from above.
        We Presbyterians, other mainline Protestants, and Catholics
            should never let ourselves be robbed of that insight
            or of that language.

Let me see if I can explain what I mean.
There's a young man from my past I'll call Tom.
Tom had a little trouble getting over fool's hill . . .
    more than a little actually.
        I happened to be there one time
            when he needed someone
            to help him pick up the pieces of his life
            and ever since,
            about once or twice a year,
            he writes me a long letter

and I write him a long letter back . . .
it's been going on for a decade or more I guess.

Tom's letters are almost always filled
with ponderous questions.
Since I have a fondness for ponderous questions
that almost equals my fondness for Tom,
I usually enjoy writing to him.

In a recent letter he said,
among many other things,

"Preacher Jim, do you ever wonder who you are . . .
I mean really who are you?"
It was not an angry question.
"I wonder that about myself sometimes," he said.

"Dear Tom," I replied,
"I want you to know I've lived long enough
to be a card-carrying graduate
of the small-group movement of the seventies.
That means I have spent an uncommon
amount of time in various small groups
pondering the very question you asked.
I'm not sure the fads of the seventies helped much
but I have come to see pretty clearly who I am.
Get ready.
Here goes:

I am a person who has come to believe
that ultimate truth is defined in and by
Jesus of Nazareth."

I didn't stop there.

"Two plus two still equals four," I said, "and that is truth.
The square root of nine is three and that is truth.
So far as I know, $E$ equals $MC^2$ just like Mr. Einstein said.

Gravity still pulls to the center of the earth
 and the law of supply and demand still applies;
 but, for me,
 ultimate truth is defined in and by Jesus of Nazareth
 and that is who I am."

Now . . .
I want you to know it felt good to say that.
Sometimes we just have to say the words.
It's what I believe it means to be born from above.
If we don't see John 3:16 in the context
 of deciding ultimate truth among all other truth,
 we might miss some of the tension and mystery of the text.
  We Presbyterians, other mainline Protestants, and Catholics
   ought not let anybody shame us out of that.
  It's also why I want to tell you about the funeral
  of Tex Malone.

The funeral director got out of the hearse, ambled around back, and opened the door. He got out two shovels and a pick, handed them to the men, and went to stand under a shade tree. The men, who no doubt had known what to expect, hung their coats on a pine sapling, took the shovels and pick, and started to dig Tex's grave. Marj and the three children joined the women who were standing beside the pickups. The women poured them glasses of iced tea. I hung my coat on the pine sapling and took my turn with the others.

We worked two at a time in the hot July Alabama sun. It was a time to tell stories about Tex. I heard about the smartest boy in the class with a mean papa who didn't care too much for his boy reading "liberry" books; and a good mama who saw that he went to Sunday school and church.

Maybe that's how Tex knew the church would always help the children no matter what.

I heard about a hard-drinking, hard-hitting young man who went to Texas to work the oil rigs. It's where he got his name and where he met Marj. When he hit bottom, he came home and drank himself to death.

When it was my turn to tell a story about Tex, I told about his last day, how Marj had called me because Tex was mighty sick. I went in my Freudian gilt Ford Maverick to pick him up and take him to the hospital just like I had done many times before; only this time neither of the hospitals in town would take him in. Both said they knew him well and, sad as it made them, there was nothing more they could do for Tex Malone. They were good people and long suffering. I did not fault them then and I do not fault them now.

Still, that left me with Tex Malone in the backseat of my new Freudian gilt Ford Maverick. Not knowing anything else to do, I drove him 120 miles to the VA hospital in Tuscaloosa. . . . Tex stretched out as best he could, alternately lying very still and praying to die and then screaming at the serpents he was seeing in his mind's eye. He was, of course, having delirium tremens owing to withdrawal from too much hard liquor.

I got Tex to the VA hospital in Tuscaloosa. He died about a half hour later. I suppose it was better than having his children listen to him scream at the serpents.

Speaking of serpents,
　　it reminds me of another part of the context of John 3:16.
It's that part of the context
　　almost nobody pays attention to anymore;
　　and for good reason.
　　　　It's hard to make any sense of it.
　　　　Just listen to it:

> *As Moses lifted up the serpent in the wilderness,*
> *so must the Son of Man be lifted up.* . . .

　　　　Then, strange to say,
　　　　　　the text launches straightway
　　　　　　into your favorite verse and mine:

> *For God so loved the world that he gave* . . .

The serpent reference
　　is to an obscure little passage in the Book of Numbers.
Since the Age of Enlightenment
　　nobody has paid much attention to it.

It's like Will Willimon said
in one of his sermons down at Calvary Church.
Since we have become enlightened
we no longer like to think of evil among us
in terms of demons and serpents and creatures like that.
The only problem is,
when we gave up that language
we didn't replace it with any other language
and it's hard now to talk about the reality of evil.[4]
Some people don't even like the fact that
we have a prayer of confession in worship every Sunday.
None of us likes to talk about evil
and we surely don't have to dwell on it endlessly,
but it's here.
All you have to do is listen to the news
and read the paper . . .
listen to the news, read the paper,
and feel the deadly depth of your own temptations.

We may no longer know what to name evil
but we need to name it something
so we can know what difference it makes
to believe in Jesus.

In the story from the Book of Numbers
when the children of God were wandering in the wilderness,
like now,
it felt like they were wandering round and round in circles
and the promises of God were far, far away.
It was as though they were being attacked by serpents.

When God delivered them from the serpents,
Moses held the bronze image of a serpent
up high on a stick
and it became for them
a symbol of God's deliverance . . .
the worst that could happen
became the symbol of their hope.

In the same way,
    for John,
    the worst that could happen
    would become the symbol of our hope.
That is,
    for John,
    and now for us,
    the cross of Jesus of Nazareth,
    symbol of the worst that evil can do,
    has become the symbol of our hope[5]

and our hope is very serious business  . . .

far more serious than a crudely printed sign
declaring "John 3:16,"
to be held up at sporting events.

No one is apt to think much of serpents and crosses
    at sporting events.
The death of Tex Malone was not a sporting event.

Neither was his funeral.

Working two at a time and swapping off every five to ten minutes, we dug Tex Malone's grave in less time than you might think. When we had the grave dug, the funeral director ambled over from the shade and backed the old Buick hearse close to the grave while we got our coats off the pine sapling, no matter that we were soaking wet with sweat. No words were spoken about the coats. That much dignity was assumed.

Hot gray smoke blew out the tailpipe of the old Buick. We rolled the pauper's casket out, and using ropes like they do in old Western movies, we lowered the casket into the grave. The casket was made of wood and covered with gray cloth to make it look like metal. It was the cheapest one you could buy but about as good as any I suppose.

With Tex in the grave, I said the words before we covered him up:

*I am the resurrection and the life,*
    *says the Lord. . . .*

*Those who believe in me,*
*even though they die,*
*yet shall they live.*

*The Lord is my shepherd I shall not want. . . .*
*Even though I walk*
*through the valley of the shadow of death,*
*I will fear no evil.*

*Who is in a position to condemn . . .*
*if God is for us, who can be against us.*

*I am sure that nothing in life*
*and nothing in death*
*can separate us from the love of God*
*in Christ Jesus our Lord.*

After I read the words, I said the prayers. After I said the prayers, I pronounced the benediction:

*The Lord give you peace*
*both now and in the life everlasting. Amen.*

I went over and touched Marj's hand and the hands of each of the children, then went to stand with the others for a few minutes before we would take off our coats again to fill the grave.

Just then Marj spoke up. It was the first she had spoken since I picked her up in my Freudian gilt Ford Maverick. "Ain't you gonna read John 3:16?" she said. "Never heard of a funeral where they didn't read John 3:16. Most folks thought Tex weren't worth shootin' but he believed that much."

"I know for a fact he believed that well," I said. "I meant him no dishonor. I'll be proud to read those words. If you would prefer it, I'd be most pleased to read them from his Bible."

She handed the Bible to me. I opened it to the right place and read from it. I'm glad to say, I thought to read at least this much of the context:

*As Moses lifted up the serpent in the wilderness,*
*so must the Son of Man be lifted up. . . .*

I kept going:

> *For God so loved the world,*
>> *that he gave his only begotten Son,*
>> *so that whosoever believeth in him should not perish,*
>> *but have everlasting life.*

And I didn't stop there:

> *For God sent not his Son into the world to condemn the world;*
>> *but that the world through him*
>> *might be saved.*

Just then, a most remarkable thing happened. As I turned to hand Marj Tex's Bible, the sun caught the sign of the cross . . . the cross on the stub of the steeple of the old abandoned church. It was like a vision or something. I'll never forget it.

I drove my Ford Maverick for many miles after that,
> but in it all,
> the backseat never was quite rid of the odor and memory
> of Tex Malone thrashing there and screaming at the serpents.
>> The odor and memory of it served to keep me knowing
>>> you don't have to die to be filled with hope;
>>> and you don't have to die for things to get better;
>>> but even in the end,
>>> there is still hope.

> It's what it means to believe in Jesus.
> It's what it means to believe ultimate truth
>> is defined in and by Jesus of Nazareth.

Idlewild Church
Fourth Sunday in Lent, 1997

# By the Waters of Babylon

By the waters of Babylon,
   there we sat down and wept,
   when we remembered Zion.
On the willows there
   we hung up our lyres.
For there our captors
   required of us songs,
and our tormentors, mirth, saying,
   "Sing us one of the songs of Zion!"

How shall we sing the LORD's song
   in a foreign land?
If I forget you, O Jerusalem,
   let my right hand wither!
Let my tongue cleave to the roof of my mouth,
   if I do not remember you,
if I do not set Jerusalem
   above my highest joy!

Remember, O LORD, against the Edomites
   the day of Jerusalem,
how they said, "Rase it, rase it!
   Down to its foundations!"
O daughter of Babylon, you devastator!
   Happy shall he be who requites you
   with what you have done to us!
Happy shall he be who takes your little ones
   and dashes them against the rock!

(Psalm 137)[1]

_____

Billy Joe Hooper lived on Dantzler Street in the house between my grandmother Banks's house and the house where they carved out an apartment for my mother and brother and me to live in while my pappy was off fighting the big war.

Some say the house where Billy Joe Hooper lived is haunted . . . haunted by the ghost of a woman who died there under mysterious circumstances. You can't prove it by me. I was never so much bothered by the ghost as I was by Billy Joe Hooper.

Oh, in time, Billy Joe Hooper and I became fast friends—went to the picture show together every Saturday along with my big brother and Junior Grier, only Junior Grier was black and had to sit in the balcony. That didn't make any more sense to me then than it does now; but that's the way things were then.

Some things change that need to be changed;
other things never change.

Anyway, when we first moved back to Saint Matthews, South Carolina, so my pappy could go fight the big war, Billy Joe Hooper was the bully of the neighborhood. I was a new kid on the block. He was probably a couple of years older. He was definitely half a head taller, a whole lot stronger, and wiser by far in the ways of Dantzler Street.

Mean is what he was. Knocked me down. Rubbed my nose in the dirt. Said bad things about my pappy . . . things I knew weren't true, and there wasn't a blessed thing I could do.

That's one of the things that never changes. Sometimes when things go wrong there's not a blessed thing you can do.

Except there was one thing I could do. I could stay awake at night plotting ways to get even . . . ways I could break not only his arms and legs, but ways I could break his back, and ways I could train our dog, Penny, and my grandmother's dog, Dopey, to become killer dogs who would lie and wait and attack the dreaded Billy Joe Hooper when he least expected it . . . no matter that Penny was only about twelve inches high and Dopey didn't have but three legs.

My five-year-old plotting was not one of my finer moments. I really have become a person committed to nonviolence; and, as I said, Billy Joe Hooper and I became fast friends. In fact, I would like nothing so much now as to hear where Billy Joe Hooper is and how he is getting on and what he's been doing for the last forty-five or fifty years. The last time I was in Saint Matthews I couldn't find anyone who knew. One of the sad things about becoming an adult is that we seldom have such friends as Billy Joe Hooper anymore, for whom raw bitterness can turn quickly to raw devotion and it is as though the bitterness were never there.

Of such is the Kingdom of Heaven. Too bad as adults we forget how to do that. At the time, though, as unthinkable as they were, my dreams of breaking Billy Joe Hooper's arms and legs and back were utterly honest.

Wonder what would have happened if I had turned my honest dreams into equally honest prayers?

> *By the waters of Babylon,*
>> *there we sat down and wept. . . .*

It starts off nobly enough:
> a sad psalm for sad people;
> a psalm for a people once held captive;
> a psalm now used for any people
> whose pain is by someone else's hand . . .
> whose pain is out of control
> and there is not a blessed thing you can do.

By psalm's end, however,
> the psalm is anything but noble:
> it becomes a mean psalm;
> a psalm for an angry people;
> a psalm for a people held captive to bitterness;
> a psalm so vicious that parts of it
> are now seldom used by any people
> no matter how resentful they are
> of their circumstance.

> *By the waters of Babylon,*
>> *there we sat down and wept,*
>> the psalm begins.
> *How shall we sing the Lord's song*
>> *in a foreign land?*
>> the psalm continues.
> But then the psalm ends:

*I pray God*
> *will dash their babies' heads against a stone.*
Worse than that.
The psalm really ends:
*I pray it will make God happy*
> *to dash their babies' heads against a stone.*

Walter Brueggemann,
> a leading Old Testament scholar of our day,
> says this psalm
> is not one of the noble moments of the Bible.[2]
That seems to me an understatement.
Walter Brueggemann, I think,
> has been too kind.
This psalm may be the very lowest moment of the Bible.
I can think of no lower moment in all of holy writ.
It's right there somewhere below
> the killing of the firstborn of Egypt
>> so Pharaoh would let God's people go
> and striking Uzzah dead
>> because he reached to keep the ark
>> from falling off the cart.

But then,
> crawling from somewhere beneath
> the dark underside of this ignoble psalm
> comes a backdoor invitation
> to a kind of prayer
> that is passionate
> in its utter honesty:
>> Prayer that is almost like
>>> the daydreams of little boys and girls
>>> confronted for the first time
>>> with stark injustice.

Our God
> will no more dash the heads of children
> than I could break the arms, legs, and back
> of Billy Joe Hooper
> or have him attacked

by a vicious three-legged dog;
but such an honest dream once helped
a little boy deal with evil
at a time when his daddy was not there to help.
    Maybe prayer that honest can also
        help God's people
        at a time when there is no other help.

Oh, to be sure,
    to dwell on such dreams and prayers,
    and certainly
    to act on such dreams and prayers,
    would be pathological;
    but have you never stayed awake half the night
    dreaming of all the caustic things
    you could have
    or even should have said to someone who caught you off guard
    and left you momentarily speechless:

        "I wish I had said . . ."
        "Next time I see him I'm going to tell him . . ."
        "Why didn't I think to say . . ."

Or,
    have you never spent hours writing a nasty letter . . .
    I mean really nasty . . .
    one that,
    if taken seriously,
    would end all injustice
    forever:

        "Madam,
            In response to your asinine statement,
                which insulted my integrity . . ."

        "Dear Sir:
            You are a disgrace to your high office
                and an impediment
                to the cause of freedom and justice . . ."

"To whom it may concern:
This is to inform you
that I am about to consult a lawyer . . ."
(That'll get 'em.)

The only time you get in trouble with letters like that
is when you mail 'em.
As long as you don't mail 'em
they can help you blow off a lot of steam.

Being able to turn such raw and honest emotion
into raw and honest prayer
is even better.
God is more understanding
than the people
to whom we might be tempted to send nasty letters:

"Lord, it will make me happy as a clam
if his new wife's pretty young face
turns into lizard leather.
She cost me my family."

"Lord, it will make me just pleased as punch
if that so-and-so corporate raider's jet
crashes into the Andes.
He cost me my job."

"Lord, it will just tickle me to death
if that dictator steps on one of his own bombs.
The carnage he preaches
inspires terrorists to plant their bombs."

I don't recommend those prayers.
As a pastor,
I don't recommend them for one minute.
I think there are better things to be praying;
but coming from the dark underside of this scandalous psalm
and from beneath our scandalous prayers
there is the voice of God
with sadness
saying,

"If they are really honest,
I will listen even to those prayers."

Coming, then,
welling up
from the top side of the psalm,
the psalmist makes it clear God is saying,
"All of your prayers
must be utterly honest."

I hadn't been out of seminary long when I had to go tell a young mother that her husband had fallen under the track of a bulldozer on the construction site where he was foreman. He was dead. I found her at the beauty parlor and had to call her out to tell her. News like that would travel like wildfire around our small community. I didn't want her to hear it from a stranger.

Standing there in the parking lot with her hair in curlers, she beat on me with both her fists. She beat on me not because she was angry with me. She beat on me because she was angry with God and I was God's representative.

It was an honest prayer.
It was a good prayer.
It was a prayer that brought healing.

*By the waters of Babylon,*
*there we sat down and wept. . . .*

and before it is over,

*Lord, bash the babies' heads against a stone.*

It is awful . . .
just awful . . .
no matter the time . . .
no matter the culture . . .
it is an unthinkably awful prayer.

Yet the signal is clear.
For us
    there is
        no pain so deep there can be no relief;
For us
    there is
        no loneliness so absolute there is no friend;
For us
    there is
        no fear so great there can be no calm;
        no death so final there can be no life;
        no grief so deep there can be no consolation;
        no injustice so insidious there can be no truth;
        no sin so serious there can be no forgiveness;
        no war so fierce there can be no peace;
        no hate so deep there can be no love;
        no conflict in the community so divisive
            there can be no understanding.

        For us
            there is
                no prayer so honest it will not be heard.

Our honest praying will not force God's hand;
    but our honest praying will bring the will of God into focus;
    and to our honest prayers God will say,

        "Here,
            let me take your bitterness from you
            and your pain.
        Now,
            come
            and follow me
            and let me show you the place of healing."

                    Idlewild Church
            Fourth Sunday in Lent, 1993

# The Colt

Rejoice greatly, O daughter Zion!
    Shout aloud, O daughter Jerusalem!
Lo, your king comes to you
    triumphant and victorious is he,
humbled and riding on a donkey,
    on a colt, the foal of a donkey.

(Zechariah 9:9)[1]

When they were approaching Jerusalem, at Bethphage and Bethany, near the Mount of Olives, [Jesus] sent two of his disciples and said to them, "Go into the village ahead of you, and immediately as you enter it, you will find tied there a colt that has never been ridden; untie it and bring it. If anyone says to you, 'Why are you doing this?' just say this, 'The Lord needs it and will send it back here immediately.'" They went away and found a colt tied near a door, outside in the street. As they were untying it, some of the bystanders said to them, "What are you doing, untying the colt?" They told them what Jesus had said; and they allowed them to take it. Then they brought the colt to Jesus and threw their cloaks on it; and he sat on it. Many people spread their cloaks on the road, and others spread leafy branches that they had cut in the fields. Then those who went ahead and those who followed were shouting,
    "Hosanna!
        Blessed is the one who comes in the name of the Lord!
        Blessed is the coming kingdom of our ancestor David!
    Hosanna in the highest heaven!"
    Then he entered Jerusalem and went into the temple; and when he had looked around at everything, as it was already late, he went out to Bethany with the twelve. (Mark 11:1–11)[2]

Who could have thought
  God would choose the colt of a donkey
  to be a noble beast of destiny?


I don't know too much about donkeys.
I have almost no personal experience with them.
As it happens, however,
  I have had quite a bit of experience with mules.

I've always liked mules. My grandfather taught me how to count
to twenty by standing at the top of a red hill of cotton and counting
the mules pulling plows in his cotton fields. That red hill is now an
island in the middle of Lake Hartwell, and my grandfather's cotton
fields are now mostly underwater. I suppose that's progress: more
progress than destiny, though I suppose in some grand scheme, making lakes out of cotton fields is a minor cog in the wheel of destiny.

On the day before Jesus was to ride into Jerusalem . . .

On the day before Jesus was to ride into the city of destiny
  he stood on the Mount of Olives
  from which he could survey the city . . .

  from which he could contemplate destiny.

    By three out of four Gospel accounts
      Jesus sent two of his disciples to fetch
      the colt of a donkey.[3]
    It's the way the Old Testament prophet had said it would be.
    Zechariah had said the colt of a donkey
      would be the beast
      to carry the Lord of life into the city of destiny.

Wonder why the colt of a donkey?

I remember once going with my grandfather to the train station
to take delivery of two new mules that had come in by cattle car.
They weren't much more than colts themselves. Living in Tennessee
as I am now proud to say, I wouldn't be surprised if those mules

came from over in Columbia, Tennessee, where, as I understand it, they once raised the finest mules in the South.

In any event, my grandfather was quite pleased to be receiving his new mules. Before we left for the station he gave me two apples and asked me to put them in the pockets of my Mackinaw coat. We rode down to the depot in his medium-blue 1941 Ford sedan with the windows rolled down no matter that it was the dead of winter. My grandfather liked fresh air.

When we got to the station, we found the mules in a temporary holding pen.

"Fine mules, Mr. Lowry," the station master said to my grandfather.

With his big gentle hand, my grandfather took an apple from my Mackinaw pocket and held it out to one of the young mules just so with the palm of his hand outstretched so the mule couldn't bite his hand even by accident. When the mule took the apple, my grandfather patted her neck gently and called her Bess. Then he told me to see if the other mule would come to me. I held out the other apple just like he had shown me. The mule came and took the apple. Her nose and lips were soft and warm.

"What do you think we should name *your* mule?" my grandfather asked.

"Let's call him Bill," I said so proud I could have popped. It was the first I knew the mule would be called mine.

"All mules need girl names," my grandfather explained. It was my first lesson in genetics though I didn't know it at the time.

"What about Melinda?" I asked. It was my favorite girl cousin's name.

"Mules listen better to names with only one syllable," my grandfather said. I didn't suspect until recently that he was not only telling me the truth about mules he was protecting me from my cousin's wrath.

"What about Sally?" I wondered.

"Sally is fine, and we can call her Sal for short." It was my first lesson in syllables though I didn't know it at the time.

"Now look in Sal's eye," my grandfather said. "See how it seems she knows something the rest of us are still trying to figure out . . . something that even if she could talk she likely wouldn't tell?"

I saw what he meant. It's the way of mules. It's a lesson you can't learn from a tractor; but that's progress, I suppose, trading in mules for tractors: . . . more progress than destiny, though trading mules for tractors might be considered a small cog in the wheel of destiny.

No matter. Until the tractors came to do the plowing and the dam was built to flood the fields, Bess and Sal and all the others were an important part of our daily lives . . . our daily lives and our livelihood.

I'm glad I had a chance to look Sal in the eye.
It helps me know now,
    as a theologian of some moderate sophistication,
    why God chose the colt of a donkey
    to be the beast of his creation
    to carry the Lord of life into the city of destiny.
        I don't know whether donkeys
            and their half-first cousins, mules,
            really do know something the rest of us don't know,
            but they sure do look like they do;
            and, in all events,
            at the time of Jesus,
            donkeys were an important part of daily life . . .
            of daily life and livelihood.

Jim Forbes is the pastor of the famous Riverside Church
    in New York.
Before that he taught preaching at Union Seminary
    in that same big and ever-so-sophisticated city.
        Jim Forbes confessed to his students
            he once got so desperate for a Palm Sunday sermon
            he told the story
            from the point of view of the donkey.[4]

        I understand the desperation:
            variations on the same theme year after year;
            each Gospel narrative so nearly the same;
            everybody knows the plot already . . .

            Jesus riding into town on the colt of a donkey;
            bystanders shouting,

"Hosanna, hosanna . . .
    save us . . . save us . . .
    blessed is he who comes
    in the name of the Lord.

Hosanna, hosanna . . .
    save us . . . save us. . . ."
    (Did you know that's
    what *hosanna* means?)

"Save us, save us."

It is a strong plea . . .
    a real plea . . .
    a hopeful plea
    pouring from the heart of daily life and livelihood;
    but where do you find a fresh new angle year after year?

You can relax.
I'm not going to try to tell the story of Palm Sunday
    from the point of view of the donkey.
        Don't forget.
        I've looked a mule in the eye
            and I know better than to try to guess
            what might go on in a mule's mind;
            but the fact remains,
            three of the four accounts of the story of Palm Sunday
            tell us that Jesus rode into Jerusalem
            on the colt of a donkey,
            and, of the three that tell about the colt of a donkey,
            Mark makes an ado of the detail.
    Since we're dealing with reading Mark's account,
        and since Mark,
        of all the Gospel writers,
        seldom makes much of an ado over details,
        when Mark makes an ado about something,
        we do well to pay attention.

Aren't you glad, then,
    I have more than a passing knowledge of mules?

    Maybe not.

The folks down at Channel 3 News called me the other day.
They were doing a follow-up story
    on a recent news event of a religious nature.
It seems the governor of Arkansas
    is unwilling to call floods and tornadoes acts of God
    as the insurance companies are wont to do.
        You may have seen the article in the paper.
        The folks at Channel 3 News wanted to know
            what I thought about the governor's position.

    I'm truly sorry we couldn't work out a time
        before the program was to air
        for them to record my views on the subject,
        though I suspect,
        as I told them on the telephone,
        my views are not particularly newsworthy
        as news is mostly deemed worthy.

        All I could have said is that,
            in matters of destiny,
            at best,
            we can see only
            as through a glass darkly.
        Then I would have tried to say that
            seeing destiny through a glass darkly
            is precisely why it is important to believe
            matters of destiny
            are ultimately determined

            by the **powers**
            of love.

That probably would not make a very good news story
    but it is the best news we have to tell.

Wonder what the governor thinks of today's beautiful weather?
I don't know how
    the God of daffodils
    and redbud blooming
    and dogwoods about to bloom
    is also the God of tornadoes, floods, and piles of debris;[5]
I don't know how
    the God of new life
    brought on the wings of weather
    is also the God who is present in death
    brought with weather's disaster;
I don't know how
    God can speak to us
    through the waters of baptism
    and through the waters of a flood;

    But I have come to believe that the God of now
    is the God of destiny
    and *all* points between;

    and I do believe that destiny is somehow determined
    by the power of God's love  . . .
    love so amazing  . . .  so divine.

      It's why Mark,
        and the others,
        wanted us to know,
        by including certain details in the narrative,
        that it was God who arranged for the colt
        to carry the Lord of life
        into the city of destiny.

Actually, Mr. Governor,
    as one who has lived through a major hurricane,
    I have less trouble understanding God in natural disaster
    than I have in understanding God in human disaster.

I don't at all understand
>how God can call up an army of people of goodwill
>to aid victims of tornadoes and floods
>and at the same time stand by
>as another army takes advantage of them.

That's not all . . .
>not near all.

I don't understand even a little
>>how the God who is present when babies are born
>>is also present when they get sick . . . very, very sick.
>I don't at all know
>>how the God who is present when young people
>>prepare to profess their faith
>>so they can belong to the church
>>is also present when young people
>>organize themselves
>>so they can belong to gangs.
>I don't at all understand
>>how the God who is present
>>when people fall hopelessly in love
>>is also present
>>when people fall hopelessly out of love;

>>but I have come to believe that the God of today
>>is the God of destiny
>>*and* every single point between;
>>and I do believe that destiny is determined
>>by the power of God's love. . . .

>>>It's why God chose a noble beast from daily life
>>>and carefully arranged
>>>for the beast from daily life
>>>to carry the Lord of life
>>>into the city of crucifixion.

There's more . . .
>always more . . .
>for lists like this there is always more . . .
>so very much more.

I don't understand how
    the God who was present
    at the signing of the Declaration of Independence
    is also present in the anarchy of Zaire.
        Pray for our missionaries.
I don't understand how
    the God who created the rain forest
    is also present for its burning.
        Pray for balance between
            development and ecology everywhere.
I don't know how
    the God who was present when
    the Berlin Wall was torn down
    is also present while people still
    hate and fear one another;

    but I do believe that the God of this moment
    is the God of forever;
    and I do believe that yesterday, today, and tomorrow
    are in the hands of love.

    It's why God carefully placed
        the colt from daily living
        to carry the Lord of life
        into the city of his resurrection  . . .
        his resurrection and ours.

Before the days of tractors, as I said, my grandfather had many mules. Though it was considerably after tractors, we actually had two mules in our immediate family. My father named one of the mules Mary. When I pointed out to him that Ma-ry has two syllables, he responded by saying that the syllables in Ma-ry are short and besides he thought Mary was smart enough to handle it.

Mary dragged logs at a sawmill my father owned for a short while. My father was right. Mary was smart. She could drag the logs without being driven. All you had to do was hook the log to her traces, say, "Come up, Mary," and Mary would drag the logs to the exact place they were needed.

Pappy didn't own the sawmill very long, but for a while, Mary was an important part of our daily lives and of our daily livelihood.

The other mule in our immediate family was Nell. Nell was a small mule . . . a colt really. My father named her for my grandmother . . . his mother-in-law. He meant it as a term of endearment for them both, though I doubt that either of them thought of it just that way.

Pappy bought Nell long, long after people had any real need for a mule; but he had a particular fondness for mules so he bought her and turned her loose in the pasture just for the fun of it . . . kind of like there are some people who don't really need a pickup truck or a great big utility station wagon but because they have a particular fondness for them they buy one anyway . . . just for the fun of it. Just so, Pappy bought Nell.

Nell was playful and great fun. In summer, brothers, cousins, and neighbors of like age would take turns boosting each other up on Nell's bare back. We'd grab her around her strong neck or by her flowing mane and off she'd go like lightning with her long ears sleek back and steady; then, at an instant known only to Nell, she would stop on a dime and throw us over her head in a graceless somersault to land in a blanket of fescue; after which she would nuzzle us to get back on and do it again.

The great trick was not to land on your head. That I did not always succeed may explain some things to you even if it did less brain damage than Nintendo.

For a season,
    that great and noble creature
    was an important part of our lives . . .
    of our lives
    and of our pleasure.
        I'm not suggesting that we all sell our cars
            and buy a mule and wagon;
            but we are missing something.

            Since we're missing something,
                be careful not to miss the point.

The point is this:

> By decree of the Lord God Almighty,
>> Creator of heaven and earth
>> and of all things great and small,
>> at a particular time
>> in a particular place
>> a particularly noble beast
>> miraculously appeared
>> to bear the Lord of life
>> into the city of your destiny . . .

> your destiny and mine.

Idlewild Church
Palm (Passion) Sunday, 1997

# And the Earth Shook

After the sabbath, as the first day of the week was dawning, Mary Magdalene and the other Mary went to see the tomb. And suddenly there was a great earthquake; for an angel of the Lord, descending from heaven, came and rolled back the stone and sat on it. His appearance was like lightning, and his clothing white as snow. For fear of him the guards shook and became like dead men. But the angel said to the women, "Do not be afraid; I know that you are looking for Jesus who was crucified. He is not here; for he has been raised, as he said. Come, see the place where he lay. Then go quickly and tell his disciples, 'He has been raised from the dead, and indeed he is going ahead of you to Galilee; there you will see him.' This is my message for you." So they left the tomb quickly with fear and great joy, and ran to tell his disciples. Suddenly Jesus met them and said, "Greetings!" And they came to him, took hold of his feet, and worshiped him. Then Jesus said to them, "Do not be afraid; go and tell my brothers to go to Galilee; there they will see me."

While they were going, some of the guards went into the city and told the chief priests everything that had happened. After the priests had assembled with the elders, they devised a plan to give a large sum of money to the soldiers, telling them, "You must say, 'His disciples came by night and stole him away while we were asleep.' If this comes to the governor's ears, we will satisfy him and keep you out of trouble." So they took the money and did as they were directed. And this story is still told among the Jews to this day. (Matthew 28:1–15)[1]

*Now, after the sabbath,*
> *toward dawn of the first day of the week,*
> *Mary Magdalene and the other Mary*
> *went to the grave . . .*
>> *and, behold,*
>>> *the earth*
>>>> *shook . . .*
>>>>> or something.

Wonder what makes the earth shake like that?

It's been three years now, almost to the day, but I remember it as if it were yesterday. It somehow fell my lot to take Pappy's clothes to the funeral home. Mama or someone had already picked them out and had them spread on the bed. Still, I couldn't resist looking in his closet.

Unlike in his son's closet, in my father's closet the shirts were hanging together in one place, suits in another, sport coats in another, ties in another, with old boxes stacked neatly on the shelf above and shined shoes in a row below.

The smell of clean laundry mixed with the smell of old boxes and the residue of cigar smoke brought back a lifetime of memories. One memory in particular stands out . . . a memory of more than forty years duration now. At least I think I was no more than eight or ten years old at the time. I was looking for something in Pappy's closet. I don't at all remember now what it was. Maybe I was looking for something he had sent me to get. In any event, tucked way back in the corner I found an old shoe box. In the shoe box, mixed with yellowing discharge papers and letters from the Department of Defense, there were some old photographs.

The photos were black and white, of course. It was before the days of color. Their edges were curled.

The photographs were of dead people . . . dead people with no clothes on. In some of the photographs, the corpses were piled on top of one another. In other photographs, the corpses were in rows. In all the photographs, the corpses were nothing but skin and bone.

I ran with the photographs to ask my mother what they were. She wiped her hands on her apron, gently took the pictures from me, looked at them with great reverence, then looked at me.

There was a pause. I took the pause to mean she was wondering if I were old enough.

After a while she said, "These were taken in a concentration camp. Your father fought in the war to make people stop doing things like that."

Then she handed the pictures back to me. There was another pause. Finally she said, "You must put the pictures back in the box and never tell your father you have seen them." I never did.

Like Jesus stone cold in the grave, for me the earth stood still that day.

*At the tomb of our Lord*
  *an angel or something*
  *descended from heaven*
  *to roll away the stone*
  *and to bring a message from God.*
    *The sight of it made the guards shake*
      *like*
      *an earthquake*
      *then stand stone still*
      *like*
      *dead men.*

Strange, isn't it, how memories string together, sometimes out of sequence and sometimes spanning a decade or two. The smell of freshly laundered shirts with a residue of cigar smoke will do that for you, especially if the smell is mixed with that of old boxes with pictures of nude corpses.

At least a decade after the discovery of the pictures, one night Pappy got a phone call from out of the blue. It was one of the men from his old army command.

Pappy was polite, as Pappy would be, but only just barely. They exchanged a few niceties about children and work and maybe the candidates for president that year. When Pappy hung up, he muttered some obscenities under his breath, slapped his leg in disgust, and walked out of the room in the fashion of his long stride.

Once again, I needed the wisdom of my mother to understand the character of my father.

"What was that about?" I asked. I was a teen by then and interested in such things.

"Your father found out that that man and several others in his command executed some German prisoners they had taken just after the war."

The earth stood still that day.

"*Fear not,*"
  *the angel said to the women.*
"*Keep them afraid,*"
  *said the high priests of conventional wisdom.*
"*Come and see the empty grave,*"
  *the messenger commanded.*
"*Say the body was stolen,*"
  *said the purveyors of logic's lunacy.*
"*Go tell the disciples that death does not have the last word,*"
  *was the message from God.*
"*We'll cover your tracks to keep them in the dark about death,*"
  *said those who wished to keep the people under control.*
    *Do you see the conflicting Easter orders?*
      *Fear not.*
      *Come see.*
      *Go tell.*
    *Those are the Easter messages from God.*
      *Fear.*
      *Deceive.*
      *Conceal.*
    *Those are the Easter messages from planet Earth.*
    *It is important to know*
      *the world need not be controlled*
      *by fear, deception, and secrecy . . .*
      *neither fear, deception, and secrecy*
      *nor their partner, death.*

Clean shirts and musty boxes were not all there was in my father's closet that brought a flood of memories. There were also the shoes arranged in a neat row. There were shoes for Sunday. They were first in line if you read them from left to right. It was important to Pappy to study every Sunday in the school of the church and to worship every Sunday in the sanctuary of the church and to work every day in the mission of the church and to pray every day to the

Lord of the church. He insisted that the church be faithful. To that end, he was faithful to the church.

Like on the day of Resurrection, by such faithfulness the earth shook.

> *As the women were running*
> *to tell the disciples what the angel said,*
> *Jesus himself stopped the women and said,*
>
> > *"Go tell the disciples*
> > *I'll meet them in Galilee*
> > *to show them*
> > *they have no need to be afraid."*

Just beside his shoes for going to church, there were shoes for going to the barn. They were second in line and just before the shoes for going to play golf.

"You boys each raise a calf," Pappy said to my older brother and me one year. "When they're fat I'll buy them from you at fair market value. Then you can send the money to Mrs. Smythe in Japan. She's a missionary over there."

For the price of two cows, in those days just after the war, by his calculation, you could send a Japanese student to seminary for a year.

We raised the calves. He bought them from us. We sent the money to Mrs. Smythe. A man went to seminary—he and a half dozen or so others after him.

The earth shook.

> *Jesus said to the women,*
> > *"Go tell the disciples*
> > *I'll meet them where they live and work*
> > *and they'll know my way is a better way . . .*
> > *a better way to live and work."*

Speaking of shoes for going to the barn, they reminded me of a time much later . . . remember how memories jump across decades . . . later when Pappy said as a spin-off of a famous proverb: "Give hungry people a meal, and they'll soon be hungry. Give them a cow and some chickens, and they'll never be hungry again."

With his considerable knowledge of such things, Pappy saw to it that hundreds of cows and thousands of chickens were given to hungry people all over the world: . . . cows and chickens and ducks and goats and sheep and rabbits and pigs and geese.[2]

By such giving the earth shook.

*As the women clung to his feet,*
  *Jesus said to them,*
    *"Go tell the disciples I'll meet them in their hometown*
    *to show them*
    *there is a lot of giving left to do."*

I was an adult somewhere past the middle of my years as I stood gazing into my father's closet, being washed in a flood of memories. I have a graduate degree in theology now. I spend up to twenty hours a week studying and writing about what I believe to be the truth of Jesus Christ. I have more than twenty-five years of preaching under my belt. Only recently, however, have I begun to see the simple complexity of the faith connections in my father's heart and mind. For him, and now for me, there is a connection between the pictures in that musty box and having his sons participate in sending students to seminary in Japan. Sending Japanese students to seminary was my father's way of assuring that what happened in those pictures never happened again. For my father, and now for me, there is a connection between the executions carried out by men under my father's command and my father's giving farm animals to hungry people. Helping hungry people feed themselves was my father's way of assuring that people need never be controlled by fear of pain and death.

So we gathered at the cemetery. It was near the eve of Easter. At the cemetery we heard the preacher read the words of Jesus: "Do not be afraid. . . . Go to Galilee. . . . There you will see me."

And the earth shook beneath our feet.

Idlewild Church
Easter, 1993

# Part 3
# Pentecost

# It Was a Warm Day in . . .

Now the whole earth had one language and the same words. And as they migrated from the east, they came upon a plain in the land of Shinar and settled there. And they said to one another, "Come, let us make bricks, and burn them thoroughly." And they had brick for stone, and bitumen for mortar. Then they said, "Come, let us build ourselves a city, and a tower with its top in the heavens, and let us make a name for ourselves; otherwise we shall be scattered abroad upon the face of the whole earth." The LORD came down to see the city and the tower, which mortals had built. And the LORD said, "Look, they are one people, and they have all one language; and this is only the beginning of what they will do; nothing that they propose to do will now be impossible for them. Come, let us go down, and confuse their language there, so that they will not understand one another's speech." So the Lord scattered them abroad from there over the face of all the earth, and they left off building the city. Therefore it was called Babel, because there the LORD confused the language of all the earth; and from there the LORD scattered them abroad over the face of all the earth. (Genesis 11:1–9)[1]

When the day of Pentecost had come, they were all together in one place. And suddenly from heaven there came a sound like the rush of a violent wind, and it filled the entire house where they were sitting. Divided tongues, as of fire, appeared among them, and a tongue rested on each of them. All of them were filled with the Holy Spirit and began to speak in other languages, as the Spirit gave them ability.

Now there were devout Jews from every nation under heaven living in Jerusalem. And at this sound the crowd gathered and was bewildered, because each one heard them speaking in the native language of each. Amazed and astonished, they asked, "Are not all these who are speaking Galileans? And how is it that we hear, each of us, in our own native language? Parthians, Medes, Elamites, and residents of Mesopotamia, Judea and Cappadocia, Pontus and Asia, Phrygia and Pamphylia, Egypt and the parts of Libya belonging to Cyrene, and visitors from Rome, both Jews and proselytes, Cretans and Arabs—in our own languages we hear them speaking about God's deeds of power." All were amazed and perplexed, saying to one another, "What does this mean?" But others sneered and said, "They are filled with new wine." (Acts of the Apostles 2:1–13)[2]

---

It was a warm day in Babylon,
    or Babel as it is known by the Jews.
The breeze blew in from the desert
    and became sultry
    as it crossed the Euphrates River.
Babylon was a magnificent city
    rising there from the badlands
    of what we now know as Iraq . . .
        a city second cousin thrice removed of Baghdad,
        a nearby municipality of similar interest and intrigue.
Babylon is now a heap of rubble
    but its ruins are so old
    they've been quite unable to discover its earliest date.[3]
No matter—
    though its poetry grew out of its history and geography,
    neither its geography nor its history
    is as important to us as its poetry:

    *By the waters of Babylon,*
        *there we sat down and wept. . . .*
    *On the willows there*
        *we hung up our lyres. . . .*[4]

    *Hark! a cry from Babylon!*
        *The noise of great destruction. . . .*
    *For the Lord is laying Babylon waste,*
        *and stilling her mighty voice.*[5]

        James Weldon Johnson,
            the black preacher and poet, called it
                *that hell-border city, Babylon.*[6]

As I was saying,
>it was a certain warm day in Babylon.

By midmorning
>the breeze that blew in from the desert
>became sultry as it crossed the river
>to blow rubbish about the cobbled streets of Babylon,
>and then the wind was lost in the body heat
>of ten thousand squawking Babylonians
>intent on the day's wheeling and dealing.

By midday
>the breeze was gone
>and the sun sent ten thousand sticky Babylonians
>to find a shady place for an afternoon nap.

Later that day
>as the sun eased
>and the Babylonians began to stir again,

>>the Lord God Almighty came sauntering into town.

>>God crossed the moat
>>>and jostled the sleepy crowd by the Ishtar Gate.
>>Unnoticed,
>>>God passed through the city from north to south
>>>down Processional Street
>>>before doubling back to turn left on Adad
>>>to cross the city's only bridge over the Euphrates;
>>>the bridge,
>>>by the way,
>>>from which the boards were removed every night
>>>to prevent the two halves of the city
>>>from stealing each other blind.[7]
>>>>The Babylonians were not lovely people.

Nevertheless,
>when God surveyed the city,
>God found the Babylonians strangely . . .

>>united.

It was a sinister union:

> Like ducks on a pond
>> united against the ugly duckling;
> Like children on the playground
>> united against a new kid in the class;
> Like neighbors in the suburbs
>> united against a home for the mentally ill.


Being held in such a union
> they had but one language
> and it with very few words.

Words like:

"Ninny, ninny, boo, boo."

Oh, without a doubt,
> while trekking through the city streets
God found the Babylonians to be of one mind
but it was a dangerous mind.

They were one:

> One like a corporation united for nothing
>> except to make a profit;
> One like a nation united for nothing
>> except its own economy.
> One like a church united for nothing
>> except to serve itself.

Being of one mind like that
> they needed but one language
> and it with few words.

Words like these:

"Just give me the bottom line."

And God did not see groups alone.
God looked at the persons of Babylon
   and saw they were not schizoid.
They were altogether together.

   They were held together:

      As an addict who is held together by nothing save addiction;
      As a bag lady who is held together by nothing save need;
      As a miser who is held together by nothing save greed.

   Being together like that
      they required only one language and it with few words.
         Words like:

      "It is mine."

In the words of one commentator,
   *they were a fearful humanity*
      *organized against the purposes of God.*[8]

Such a dreadful league could not be tolerated.
So when God saw
   the sin-soaked city of Babylon,
   according to the story,
   God confused their language
   and scattered the people
   to the four corners of the earth.
      They were no longer
         one people
         of one mind
         held together
         in their acts of crime.
      They became many people
         with many tongues
         and many words.

And in our tradition
   that's the story
   of why there are so many words
   in so many languages.

I read the other day where
    the new Oxford English Dictionary
    requires a three-foot pile of very thin paper
    and extremely fine print
    to define the words in our language alone.
We must add to that, of course,
    German, French, Spanish, Japanese, Chinese, Russian, Greek,
    and all the rest
    plus all their dialects.

        Understanding truth
            with so many words in so many languages
            can be quite a riddle.

It was a warm day in Jerusalem.
The wind that blew in from the desert
    was parched and dry
    causing dust to settle on eyebrows and eyelashes
    and crust at the children's nostrils.
Jerusalem is a city
    whose history is more important to us than its poetry
    but its poetry is beautiful all the same
    to us:

        *For Zion's sake I will not keep silent,*
        *and for Jerusalem's sake I will not rest,*
        *until her vindication goes forth as brightness.*[9]

        *O Jerusalem, Jerusalem, killing the prophets*
            *and stoning those who are sent to you!*
        *How often would I have gathered your children together*
            *as a hen gathers her brood under her wings,*
        *and you would not!*[10]

        How does the modern anthem go?
        *Jerusalem, Jerusalem,*
            *lift up your gates and sing*
        *Hosanna in the highest.*
        *Hosanna to your king.*

As I was saying,
    it was a certain warm day in Jerusalem.
A holiday.
Pentecost, to be exact.
It was many, many, many years after
    that certain warm day in Babylon.

      Remember how
         a thousand years in the sight of God
         are but as yesterday when it is passed?
      That's the way it was.

By midmorning
    the breeze that blew in from the desert
    had parched every lip in town
    and sent tourists and local hucksters alike
    to the wells
    to vie with camels, sheep, and goats
    for what muddy water was there.
On holidays
    strangers came from everywhere:
        Galileans, Parthians, Medes, Elamites;
        residents of Mesopotamia, Judea, and Cappadocia;
        Egypt, Libya, Pamphylia, and all the rest.

      It was the scattered languages of Babylon
        full blown and
        come home to roost.

Ten thousand visitors squawking
    a million words
    in a hundred languages and dialects
    all intent on doing the holiday right.
By midday
    the breeze was gone
    and the sun sent ten thousand babbling tourists
    to find a shady place to rest.

Later that day
    as the sun eased
    and the tourists began to stir again,

      the Lord God Almighty came strolling into town.

God entered by the Damascus Gate
    and made way to the Temple
    to watch the religious gyrations put on for the holiday.
Soon bored with that,
    God ambled through the streets,
    like going from the cathedral to Macy's at Christmastime,
    to see the real holiday gyrations
    of the real visitors to Jerusalem.

What God heard was more important
    than what God saw:

      What God heard was like Arabs and Jews
        trying to discuss the Holy Land;
      It was like Catholics and Protestants
        trying to discuss the future of Northern Ireland;
      It was like blacks and whites
        trying to discuss the politics of South Africa;
      It was like the president and Congress
        trying to discuss health care.
      It was like Democrats and Republicans
        trying to discuss the national debt;
      It was like the school board
        trying to discuss the annual budget.

        There were too many words . . .
          words no one cared to hear
          and no one wished to understand.

God walked through the streets of Jerusalem
    to see what God could see
    or hear what God could hear:

It was like children
    trying to divide candy;
It was like couples
    trying to discuss money;
It was like parents and teens
    trying to discuss sex and curfews;
It was like divorcees
    trying to discuss the children
    and the grandfather clock;
It was like bureaucrats
    trying to explain their forms.

        There were too many words . . .
           words no one cared to hear
           and no one wished to understand.

Did it make God angry
    or did it make God sad
    to stroll the streets of Jerusalem?

        I think sad.
        Some say mad.

No matter.
The Lord God Almighty left Jerusalem,
    slump-shouldered,
    through the Damascus Gate.
But God wasn't long gone.

As it happened, the disciples of Jesus
    were together that day . . .
    together in one spot . . .
    grieving his loss perhaps
    and probably
    reflecting on what Jesus had taught them to think
    and do
    and be.

And as they reflected on one Jesus of Nazareth,

> suddenly there came
> a sound from heaven
> like the rush of a mighty wind
> and it filled the house
> with the spirit of Jesus Christ.

God wasn't long gone.
To Jerusalem,

> God gave the Spirit of
> > Love and Joy and Peace . . .
> the Spirit of
> > Touch and Forgiveness and Gentleness . . .
> at Jerusalem God gave the Spirit of

> > T r u t h.

> > And they all heard it.
> > They all heard the truth of God
> > > in his own language or
> > > in her own language.

> With the Spirit of Jesus blowing among them
> > all the people came together

> and in the Spirit of Jesus Christ
> they were able to hear each other . . .
> and to understand each other
> and to love each other.

> > It was Babylon gone full cycle.
> > It was confused language redeemed
> > > and made whole.
> > It was scattered people reunited.

> > > They called it the birth of the church.

The church has not always
    lived up to the reputation of its noble birth,
    but when,
    in the Spirit of Jesus Christ,
    the people are able to listen to each other
    and hear each other
    and love each other
        it is church.

Remember how a thousand years
    in the sight of God
    are but as yesterday
    when it is past.
Keep that in mind.

It was a warm day in Memphis, Tennessee.
The wind that blew across the Mississippi River was damp
    but pleasing.
By midmorning the rush-hour traffic was over.
At midday everyone broke for lunch.

Just as they began to stir after lunch

    the Lord God Almighty came moseying down Union Avenue

    to see what God could see.

What God heard is far more important than what God saw.

What God heard was like . . .

Idlewild Church
Pentecost Sunday, 1993

# From the Barrens

These are the descendants of Shem. When Shem was one hundred years old, he became the father of Arpachshad two years after the flood; and Shem lived after the birth of Arpachshad five hundred years, and had other sons and daughters.

When Arpachshad had lived thirty-five years, he became the father of Shelah; and Arpachshad lived after the birth of Shelah four hundred three years, and had other sons and daughters.

When Shelah had lived thirty years, he became the father of Eber; and Shelah lived after the birth of Eber four hundred three years, and had other sons and daughters.

When Eber had lived thirty-four years, he became the father of Peleg; and Eber lived after the birth of Peleg four hundred thirty years, and had other sons and daughters.

When Peleg had lived thirty years, he became the father of Reu; and Peleg lived after the birth of Reu two hundred nine years, and had other sons and daughters.

When Reu had lived thirty-two years, he became the father of Serug; and Reu lived after the birth of Serug two hundred seven years, and had other sons and daughters.

When Serug had lived thirty years, he became the father of Nahor; and Serug lived after the birth of Nahor two hundred years, and had other sons and daughters.

When Nahor had lived twenty-nine years, he became the father of Terah; and Nahor lived after the birth of Terah one hundred nineteen years, and had other sons and daughters.

When Terah had lived seventy years, he became the father of Abram, Nahor, and Haran.

Now these are the descendants of Terah. Terah was the father of Abram, Nahor, and Haran; and Haran was the father of Lot. Haran died before his father Terah in the land of his birth, in Ur of the Chaldeans. Abram and Nahor took wives; the name of Abram's wife was Sarai, and the name of Nahor's wife was Milcah. She was the daughter of Haran the father of Milcah and Iscah. Now Sarai was barren; she had no child.

Terah took his son Abram and his grandson Lot son of Haran, and his daughter-in-law Sarai, his son Abram's wife, and they went out together from Ur of the Chaldeans to go into the land of Canaan; but when they came to Haran, they settled there. The days of Terah were two hundred five years; and Terah died in Haran.

Now the LORD said to Abram, "Go from your country and your kindred and your father's house to the land that I will show you. I will make of you a great nation, and I will bless you, and make your name great, so that you will be a blessing. I will bless those who bless you, and the one who curses you I will curse; and in you all the families of the earth shall be blessed." (Genesis 11:10—12:3)[1]

---

According to our tradition,
    when Noah's son Shem was a hundred years old
Shem's wife gave birth to a son.
    They named the son Arpachshad.
    Shem lived another 500 years after that.

        It's our way of saying
           God was there.
        History was moving on
           with the people of God
           somehow at the heart of history.

        Weaving world history
           with the history of God's people
           is a very important thing for God's people to do.

        In the 1910s, for example,
           this nation was at war with much of the world.
               We fought in trenches mostly
               and against mustard gas.
               It left some barren spots in our lives and world;
                   but, for better or worse,
                   the church was there
                   binding up the wounds.

When Arpachshad was thirty-five years old
    his wife gave birth to a son.
        They named their son Shelah.
        After that, Arpachshad lived another 403 years.

        God was still there.
        History moved on
            with the people of God at the heart of history.

        As in the 1920s
            when the well-to-do among us played a lot.
                All the while the gangsters flourished.
                It left some barren spots;
                    but in the church
                    missionaries were on the move.

When Shelah was thirty years old
    Shelah's wife gave birth to a son.
        They named their son Eber.
        After that Shelah lived another 403 years.

        God was there.
        History moved on
            with the people of God firmly in the will of God.

        As in the 1930s
            when almost all of us were poor.
                There was a kind of regrouping
                    remembered now almost fondly.
                Still, the poverty of it all left some barren spots;
                    but the church was there
                    serving up the soup.

When Eber was thirty-four years old
    his wife gave birth to a son.
        They named their son Peleg.
        After that Eber lived another 430 years.

God was there.
History moved on
    with the people of God still holding forth in the midst of it all.

      As in the 1940s
          when we were at war with the world again  . . .
          the world and its insidious prejudice.
             This time we fought with big bombs.
             It left some barren spots;
                but afterward the church experienced
                its greatest growth ever.

When Eber's son Peleg was thirty years old
    Peleg's wife gave birth to a son.
      They named their son Reu.
      After that Peleg lived a scant 209 years.

      The point is,
          God was there.
      It is our tradition's way of saying
          history moved on
          with the people of God intact.

      As in the 1950s
          when we fought a little and played a lot.
             While we played, ugliness festered.
             It left some barren spots;
                but the church continued
                in a kind of revival.

When Reu was thirty-two years old
    his wife gave birth to a son.
      They named their son Serug.
      After that Reu lived only 207 years.

      But God was there.
      History moved on
          with the people of God in focus with a job to do.

As in the 1960s
>when the festering ugly spots of the fifties erupted.
>>We fought abroad
>>and we fought among ourselves.
>>It left some barren spots;
>>>but the church as it fought with itself
>>>was honing its identity.

When Serug was thirty years old
>Serug's wife gave birth to a son.
>>They named their son Nahor.
>>After that Serug lived an even 200 years.

>>The faith said God was there.
>>The faith also said God was in history
>>>holding God's people together
>>>with an important identity.

>As in the 1970s
>>when our lost innocence came into clear focus.
>>>Shame covered the highest office
>>>>of our once proud land.
>>>It left some barren spots;
>>>>but in the church we were regrouping
>>>>and a sleeping giant was beginning to wake.

When Nahor was twenty-nine years old
>his wife gave birth to a son.
>>They named their son Terah.
>>After that Nahor lived to a youthful 119.

>>Do you see how
>>>from the very beginning
>>>they wanted us to believe God was there?
>>They wanted us to see God was in their history and ours
>>>nurturing us to be the people of God.

>As in the 1980s
>>when from great prosperity came
>>>unimaginable poverty.

On that and other fronts our moral fiber
became threadbare.
It left some barren spots;
and the church . . .

well the church is right here
across the threshold
and into the 1990s,
moving headlong to a new millennium;
and where are we?

When Terah was a ripe seventy years old
his wife gave birth to a son.
They named their son Abram.
Abram was later to be better known as Abraham.
Abram married Sarai.
Sarai was later to be better known as Sara.

*Abraham and Sara . . .*

*were **barren.**[2]*

For the people of God,
history was over.
From these barren ones
it was made most clear:

*There was no future for the people of God.*

No future at all . . . no future . . . no future . . .
only a horrible present;

except, of course,

for this odd

command of God . . .

this command that has about it
the promise of a gift.

> The command of God
> to Abraham and Sara was this:
> **Move!**
> Go to the land of my promise.
> The gift of God to Abraham and Sara was this:
> I will bless you
> and make of you a blessing.

I think I shall never lose the memory of the afternoon of September 22, 1989. In some ways it is more vivid even than the night of September 21. That's the night Hurricane Hugo made landfall centered not more than a quarter mile from our Sullivan's Island home near Charleston, South Carolina. At first light, I surveyed the damage to my mother-in-law's house. That's where we weathered the storm. It's a hundred and forty miles inland as the crow flies. The terrain was dismal, but damage to the house was minimal. I then made my way among the fallen trees the mile or so to my parents' house to survey the damage there. I helped my dad board up a window that had blown in. I also went with him to find some men with chain saws. I stayed long enough to see that the men would be able to clear my parents' drive.

As soon as I could, and glad I had filled my car with gas the night before, I left Martha with her mother and headed home. Whatever was there, the church had to be the church and I could at least call the church together. In Columbia, without slowing down, thanks to the miracles of modern technology, I was able to call our daughters in Florida on the car phone to let them know we were all right.

South and east of Orangeburg, South Carolina, the damage started to get worse and worse. In some places only one lane was clear on the interstate. That was enough. There was almost no traffic.

In the outskirts of Charleston the warehouses along the highway were crumbled or crumbling, but the worst was yet to come. The image that is fixed forever in the front of my memory is the picture that Friday from the Cooper River Bridge. The Cooper River Bridge connects the peninsula of Charleston to Mount Pleasant and points north. Mount Pleasant is where the church I was serving is located. The bridge rises high above the harbor and gives a panoramic view of

Mount Pleasant, and then goes on to Sullivan's Island, which is where we lived. Mine was the only car on the bridge just then.

For no reason, at least none that has any claim to logic, I drove across the bridge at seventy-five or eighty miles per hour. I know that because that's as fast as my little car could go. Do you suppose I was trying to run to or from what was ahead?

In the ensuing weeks I saw that picture of Mount Pleasant and Sullivan's Island a hundred times and more; but the first time was the worst time.

You see, there was nothing left in our town that was green. Nothing. Everything green was gone. The scant trees left standing had been stripped of their leaves.

Ours was a barren land.
Ours was a land
   for which history
   had come to a sudden
   and abrupt
   halt.
      There was for us no future.
      There was for us only
         a horrible and frightening present:

No future at all . . . no future . . . no future . . .

    except, of course,

    for this odd

        command of God . . .
           this command that has about it
           the promise of a gift.

      "Go to my promise," says God.
      "I will bless you
         and make of you a blessing."

Which is, of course,
    exactly what happened.

The command of God is this:

Move!
In faith,
    move from your hopelessness.

    So from that barren land
        we moved in faith to rebuild our lives and town.
    You will want to know
        that it was the church of Jesus Christ
        that was the first and lasting source of sanity
        to meet the emergency and to rebuild lives.

    No denominational turf building . . .
    No doctrinal hairsplitting . . .
    No ecclesiastical infighting . . .
    No political position jockeying . . .
    No bureaucratic paper shuffling . . .

        just the Body of Jesus Christ
            rising out of the mud:
                to house people by the thousands;
                to feed people by the tens of thousands;
                to haul debris and muck by the ton;
                to dry an ocean of tears;
                to hug everybody in sight; and
                to worship . . . oh yes, to worship
                as few of us had ever worshiped before.

From that once barren land
    the church of Jesus Christ claimed
        the promise of our God:

        *I will bless you*
            *and make of you a blessing.*

People of God, it happened.

I no longer think God speaks to us
> from the barren places of our lives only.
Rather, I have come to think
> simply that it is from the barren places of our lives
> that we hear God most clearly:

> From the cross Jesus said,
>> "Father, forgive them. . . ."[3]
>>> In the terror of it
>>>> we cannot miss the meaning of forgiveness.
> To the quarreling church Paul wrote,
>> "Love is patient; love is kind. . . ."[4]
>>> In the contrast of it
>>>> we cannot miss the heart of love.
> To the persecuted church John wrote,
>> "I saw a new heaven and a new earth. . . ."[5]
>>> Against such hopelessness,
>>>> we cannot miss the meaning of hope.

For your reflection
> may I suggest you do just this:

> Think of the broad sweep of your world.
> Consider especially the barren places
>> where your world's history seems threatened
>>> by its present.

>> Is there nothing but barren hopelessness
>>> for the lands of ethnic fighting?

>> Is the human spirit so barren in the lands of famine
>>> that not even the children can be fed
>>> except when there is the sheer force
>>> of goodwill?

The cost of freedom
   is leaving a barren path
   through too many places just now:
      Eastern Europe;
      the countries of the former Soviet Union;
      the Middle East;
      Central America.

Does it not strike terror in your heart
   that as communism dies
   the barren plane of fascism rises
   on the horizon?

Must the space between races
   forever be barren space?

Is the religious community powerless
   to combat the barren emptiness of fanaticism
   even when it strikes fear as close to home
   as Oklahoma City?

Listen ever so carefully.
It is from just such barren places
   that the command of God
   can be heard most clearly
   by the people of God.

The command of God is this:
   Move!
   Move from your hopelessness.
   Move in faith.
   Move to my promise.

The promise of God is a gift.
The gift of God is this:
   I will bless you
      and make of you a blessing.
   It works.
   It works!

Who has not been inspired
as the religious community in
Oklahoma City has risen from the rubble
to bring sanity and healing!

Consider also for your devotional thought
the broad sweep of your own history
and the barren places of your own life:

Is there something going on in your family
that has left you wondering where to go and what to do?
Is there some deep longing
that has left you depressed and empty?
Is there some deep anger
that has claimed all your energy?
Is there some fear
that has trapped your imagination?
Is there some addiction
that has captured your will?
Is there some perversion
that has taken charge of your good judgment?

From wherever your barren place might be
listen ever so carefully to the command
of your God.

The command of your God is this:
Move!
Move from your hopelessness.
Move in faith.
Move to the place of my promise.

The promise of God is this:
I will bless you
and make of you a blessing.

When Abraham was 100 years old,
    from Sara's barren womb
    a son was born to Abraham and Sara.
        They named their son Isaac.
To Isaac and his wife, Rebekah,
    twin sons were born.
        They named their sons Esau and Jacob.
From Jacob,
    who was later named Israel,
    twelve tribes were formed.
From one of the tribes of Israel
    came the house of King David.
In due season,
    in the city of David,
    to you a Savior was born.

Calvary Church, Memphis
Season of Pentecost, 1995

# These Who Darken Counsel

Then the LORD answered Job out of the whirlwind:
    "Who is this that darkens counsel by words without knowledge?
Gird up your loins like a man,
    I will question you, and you shall declare to me.

"Where were you when I laid the foundation of the earth?
    Tell me, if you have understanding.
Who determined its measurements—surely you know!
    Or who stretched the line upon it?
On what were its bases sunk,
    or who laid its cornerstone
when the morning stars sang together
    and all the heavenly beings shouted for joy?"
                                   (Job 38:1–7)[1]

Jesus called them and said to [the disciples], "You know that among the Gentiles those whom they recognize as their rulers lord it over them, and their great ones are tyrants over them. But it is not so among you; but whoever wishes to become great among you must be your servant, and whoever wishes to be first among you must be slave of all. For the Son of Man came not to be served but to serve, and to give his life a ransom for many." (Mark 10:42–45)[2]

----

Hear this question from God:

*Who are these who darken counsel?*
*Who are these who dare to question God . . .*
*who dare to wonder what and how . . .*
*and sometimes even*
*to wonder why?*

And hear this message from the Son of God:

*Whoever would be first among you*
*must be servant of all.*

Mr. O. T. Walenczky[3] was a faithful servant of the church . . . servant of the church and mostly of the God of the church. He lived in a small southern town. The little town where Mr. Walenczky lived is a lot like Mitford, the imaginary town in Jan Karon's delightful four-part series of novels about Father Tim, the Episcopal priest, and the cast of town characters: Dooley, Father Tim's adopted son; Puny, the housekeeper; Mule Skinner, the town character; and, of course, Cynthia, Father Tim's late-in-life true love. If you've read any or all of the novels, you know there is no place this side of heaven that is exactly like Mitford, but Mr. Walenczky's little town is about as close as you can get.

In his spare time Mr. Walenczky hung out at the First Presbyterian Church and fixed things that were broken. He had reached the age when most of his time was spare, so he was at First Church often.

Actually, I'm not sure why they call it First Presbyterian. There's not apt to be another Presbyterian church in that town until the neighboring city overruns it.

No matter. Mr. Walenczky was a faithful servant of First Presbyterian Church . . . servant of the church but mostly of the God of the church. He replaced worn-out electrical switches. He fixed leaky faucets. He built playground equipment and puppet stages. He reglued Sunday School chairs and repainted Sunday School rooms. All the people at First Church loved Mr. Walenczky.

One day, as a surprise to everyone, Mr. Walenczky showed up with a much-needed new sign to go in front of the church. It was truly a work of art and must have taken him months to plan and build. Its design blended perfectly with the architecture of the lovely church building. Each letter was flawlessly cut from fine wood and fastened on an elegant background. The times of services were thoughtfully and tastefully arranged toward the bottom. It was all encased in glass and effectively but discreetly lighted as Presbyterians would want their sign lighted.

In short, the sign was the work of a professional and it saved the church thousands of dollars.

There was, however, one problem. Mr. Walenczky misspelled *Presbyterian.* He left out the *i.*

Actually, by leaving out the *i,* it left the word not much unlike the way he pronounced it: *Presbyteran.* . . . "We're Presbyterans, don't you know?"

But let me tell you the wonderful thing . . . let me tell you the thing that is absolutely filled with wonder . . . filled with wonder and grace: As long as he lived, nobody in that whole congregation ever told Mr. Walenczky about his error! It was like the whole congregation rose up and, without a formal plan at all, became the servant of the servant and did no less nor more than proclaim the beauty of the sign. For years they endured the ridicule of their neighbors who met them in the drug store or the IGA and said, "Hey, what's the matter with you 'Presbyterans,' can't you spell?" Still, no one breathed a word to Mr. Walenczky.

That's the church at its best.

I took the story from a particular congregation; but there are people just like Mr. Walenczky all over most congregations; and for all the warts covering the church, most congregations are filled with people who wouldn't dare correct his spelling.

*Whoever would be first among you*
*must be servant of all.*
*The Son of Man came also to serve*
*and not to be served.*

But hear this again also:

*Who are these who darken counsel?*
*Who are these who dare to question God . . .*
*who dare to wonder what and how . . .*
*and sometimes even*
*to wonder why?*

Sometimes I wonder why,
don't you?
So did Mr. Walenczky.

For a while the little church in the little southern town had a special ministry to some folks in special need of love. On the edge of town, the state prison system had a work-release center where young male offenders could spend the last few months of their sentences while they took jobs in the community. On Sundays, by special arrangement, several families in the congregation would invite young men from the work-release center to come to worship with them and then to go home with them after worship for Sunday dinner. Mr. and Mrs. Walenczky were among the regulars who participated in the ministry. In fact, they became quite attached to one particular young man. He was nice looking, clean cut, soft spoken, playful; he could have been one of their grandsons.

On a particular Sunday afternoon I got a call from one of the Walenczky's neighbors saying the young man had held the Walenczkys at bay with a kitchen knife. The neighbor said Mr. and Mrs. Walenczky were alright but the young man had made off with their silverware and Mrs. Walenczky's jewelry some of which had been brought by her grandmother all the way from the old country.

Straightway I went over and found them stunned, sitting side by side on the sofa holding hands.

"Why would God let something like this happen?" Mr. Walenczky asked his preacher.

"Honey, you know he's addicted to illegal drugs," answered Mrs. Walenczky for me.

"Why would God let a child get hooked on drugs?" Mr. Walenczky asked his preacher.

"I don't know," I said. "I'll ask God that question this very night and I'll let you know if God comes up with a half-good answer."

We left it at that, except we did pray for the young man.

You guessed it. The very next Sunday there were Mr. and Mrs. Walenczky in their usual place with a new young man from the work-release center seated between them.

> *Who are these who darken counsel?*
> *Who are these who dare to question God . . .*
> *who dare to wonder what and how . . .*
> *and sometimes even*
> *to wonder why?*
> It's the question God asked Job
> when Job dared wonder why he had suffered so.

"Who are you to wonder why?"
God answered Job's question with a question.

*Where were you*
*when I laid the foundations of the earth?*

Since that time,
    as best we can,
    when we dare to wonder why,
    in the church,
    we do our wondering
    in great reverence

(don't we?);

    and that is who we are
    in the church. . . .

      When we're at our best,
        we are a people who are not afraid to wonder why;
        but we do our wondering
        in great devotion.

That's not all.
When the time was right,
    there came yet another answer to the timeless question:

      *The Son of Man came not to be served*
        *but to serve . . .*
        *that,*
      *and to give his life as a ransom for many.*

This is who we are,
    isn't it?
We are also a community of people
    who ask the hard questions:
      In reverence and hope,
        we ask, how can it be thus?

In reverence and hope,
    we question, why is it so?
In great reverence and faithful hope,
    we wonder, who is God?

We will settle for no easy answers;
    and yet . . .
    and yet
    we know we are also called to serve;
    and in serving . . .

    we have found
    and yet find

    the truth of God.

Margaret Benjamin[4] was a stately woman of limited means, keen intellect, and great curiosity. Everyone called her Benny. She and her late husband had been schoolteachers, which left her in retirement to a simple but dignified style of living that she thoroughly enjoyed in the little southern town that is at least a little like Mitford. Benny's statuesque demeanor came more from character than good grooming. All of her gray hair seldom found its way into the bun she wore on the back of her head, leaving wisps here and there to be endlessly brushed from her face.

But let me tell you about Benny. When anyone in the congregation turned up ill, whether at home or hospital, Benny made it her practice to take them a single flower that she had grown in her garden—either a single bloom like a daffodil or an iris or a rose or sometimes it was a single small stem carefully trimmed from a flowering shrub like jasmine or azalea or camellia. If the sick person happened to be a woman or girl, Benny pinned the flower to her pillow. If the sick person happened to be a man or boy, she left it in a paper cup. As often as not, when I called on the sick members of the congregation, the telltale flower revealed that Benny had beat me there. Benny was, in every sense, a servant of the people.

Then one day, many years after I had moved on from that congregation, as the story was told to me, Benny had a stroke. They say it affected her speech and her right side. She was right-handed. My friend who became the pastor there after me said when he saw her in the intensive care unit she scribbled a note with her left hand. It was just one word but it spoke volumes. The word was *why.*

He didn't know why. I wouldn't have known either.

But listen to this. A few days later, as the story goes, when they moved her out of intensive care, word spread like wildfire through the congregation. Within hours, her room was covered in flowers. As I understand it, the nurses could scarcely get in the room. The whole congregation became servant to the servant.

> *Who are these who darken counsel?*
> *Who are these who dare to question God . . .*
> *who dare to wonder what and how . . .*
> *and sometimes even*
> *to wonder why?*

That was the question from God for Job . . .
for Job and for us.
It came from God as from a whirlwind;
and comes yet just so.

Then came the answer
and the answer always comes:

*God is God.*

But hold on.
In time came another answer:

> *Whoever would be first among you*
> *must be servant of all.*
> *The Son of Man came*
> *to be servant of all*
> *and to give his life*
> *as a ransom for many.*

In the church,
when we are really being the church,
we don't know why
the dog sometimes bites;

nor at all
why the bee sometimes stings;

but we do know there is nothing quite so nice
as having a dog to welcome you home;
and there is nothing quite so sweet
as honey.

We don't know why
people of different races
sometimes call each other ugly names.
We don't know why
Arabs and Jews in the Holy Land can't make peace
nor Presbyterians and Catholics in Northern Ireland.
We don't know why
people fall out of love
or children hurt one another at school;

but we do know how wonderful it is
to love and be loved.

We don't know why
some babies are born poor
and others are abused.
We don't know why
some children get very, very sick
and some grownups, too, before their time.
We don't know why
we need to have guards in the parking lot at church;

but we are bold to wonder . . .

and in our wondering
we want to be very, very reverent . . .

reverent toward the God who is . . .
the God who is

and who promises hope.

In the meantime,
> by serving each other in the name of Christ
> and by serving the city in the name of Christ,
> we have found
> and are finding the truth of God;

> and the truth of God lives among us
> and lives in us.

Idlewild Church
Season of Pentecost, 1997

# Notes

### Introduction

1. Charles Wesley, "Love Divine, All Loves Excelling."

### Low-Back, Ladder-Back, Cane-Bottom Chair with the Legs Cut Off Just So

1. Philippians 4:4–7 is the epistle listed for the third Sunday of Advent, year C, in *The Revised Common Lectionary (RCL)* (Nashville: Abingdon Press, 1992).

2. Luke 1:47–55 is listed as the psalm for the third Sunday of Advent in years A and B, and for the fourth Sunday of Advent, year C, in the *RCL*.

3. For more information about Paul's use of guard imagery, see Fred B. Craddock, *Philippians,* Interpretation: A Bible Commentary for Teaching and Preaching (Atlanta: John Knox Press, 1985), 71–72.

4. Antoine de Saint Exupéry, *The Little Prince,* trans. Katherine Woods (New York: Harcourt Brace Jovanovich, 1943), 76–78.

### Mary's Song

1. Luke 1:39–45, with verses 46–55 optional, is the Gospel reading for the fourth Sunday of Advent, years B and C; Luke 1:39–57 is the Gospel reading for the Visitation of Mary to Elizabeth (May 31) in years A, B, and C in the *RCL*.

2. Fred B. Craddock, *Luke,* Interpretation: A Bible Commentary for Teaching and Preaching (Atlanta: John Knox Press, 1990), 29.

### Listening for the Christmas Angel

1. Matthew 1:18–25 is the Gospel reading listed for the fourth Sunday of Advent, year A, in the *RCL*. I have added verses 1–17 for homiletical reasons.

2. A well-known pastor of a megachurch in Memphis has started a letter-writing campaign to encourage impeachment and conviction of President Clinton.

3. The story of Megan and its punch line were reported by Christine Chakoian in an excellent paper on the text presented to the 1998 meeting of the Movable Feast.

4. Chakoian's treatment of the righteousness issue in the biblical text was extremely helpful.

5. Someone has willfully taken and absconded with my copy of Raymond Brown's monumental *Birth of the Messiah*. I am almost positive I am indebted to Brown for this insight.

### Like the Serpent in the Wilderness

1. Numbers 21:4–9 is the Old Testament lesson listed for the fourth Sunday in Lent, year B, in the *RCL*.

2. John 3:14–21 is the Gospel lesson listed for the fourth Sunday in Lent, year B, in the *RCL*. I altered this for homiletical reasons.

3. Jon Walton quoted Ernest Campbell from the Fosdick Convocation of a few years ago. Walton's quote is in a paper he presented to the 1997 meeting of the Movable Feast.

4. Willimon preached in Memphis for the Preaching Series at Calvary Episcopal Church during Lent of 1997. His sermon was untitled.

5. Brueggemann et al. have a helpful article on the Numbers passage in *Texts for Preaching: A Lectionary Commentary Based on the NRSV, Year B* (Atlanta: Westminster/John Knox Press, 1993). The article carefully treats how the text stands on its own but becomes a *type* for John's reference to the cross. See pages 221ff.

### By the Waters of Babylon

1. Psalm 137 is an alternate psalm listed for the twenty-second Sunday of Ordinary Time, year C, in the *RCL*. Other lectionaries list only verses 1–6. This translation of the psalm is from the Revised Standard Version.

2. Walter Brueggemann, *The Message of the Psalms: A Theological Commentary* (Minneapolis: Augsburg Publishing House, 1984). See pages 74ff.

### The Colt

1. Zechariah 9:9, which is not listed as a Lenten text in the *RCL*, was read for homiletical reasons.

2. Mark 11:1–11 is listed as an alternate psalm for Palm (Passion) Sunday, year B, in the *RCL*.

3. The Gospel of John makes no mention of the colt.

4. Neta Pringle recounted this story about her preaching professor in a paper she presented to the 1997 meeting of the Movable Feast. I am grateful for this and many other contributions to this sermon she provided in her excellent presentation.

5. As this sermon was being preached, the Mississippi River, which forms the western border of Tennessee and of Memphis, had just begun to recede from a high mark that has not been exceeded since 1937.

### And the Earth Shook

1. Matthew 28:1–10 is the Gospel reading listed for Easter, year A, in the *RCL*. I added verses 11–15 for homiletical reasons.

2. My father served for many years on the board of directors of Heifer Project International.

### It Was a Warm Day in . . .

1. Genesis 11:1–9 is the Old Testament lesson listed for the day of Pentecost, year C, in the *RCL*.

2. Acts of the Apostles 2:1–21 is an alternate reading for the day of Pentecost for years A, B, and C in the *RCL*.

3. George A. Buttrick, ed., *The Interpreter's Dictionary of the Bible: An Illustrated Encyclopedia,* vol. 1 (Nashville: Abingdon Press, 1962), 334.

4. Psalm 137:1–2, RSV.

5. Jeremiah 51:54–55, RSV.

6. James Weldon Johnson, *God's Trombones: Seven Negro Sermons in Verse* (New York: Viking Press, 1927), 25.

7. Buttrick, *Interpreter's Dictionary of the Bible,* 335–336.

8. Walter Brueggemann, *Genesis,* Interpretation: A Bible Commentary for Teaching and Preaching (Atlanta: John Knox Press, 1982), 100. Those familiar with Brueggemann's commentary will recognize his work in much of this sermon, both in its Genesis and its Acts sections. As usual I am grateful for Professor Brueggemann's insight and sensitivity.

9. Isaiah 62:1, RSV.

10. Luke 13:34, RSV.

### From the Barrens

1. Genesis 12:1–9 appears during the season of Pentecost as Proper 5, year A, in the *RCL*. For homiletical reasons I added 11:10–29 to the reading and omitted 12:4–9.

2. I am grateful yet again for the insight of Walter Brueggemann. In his commentary *Genesis,* he treats 11:30—12:9 as a unit, for the logical reason that Abraham and Sara's barrenness stands in stark interruption of the context in which it is related. See pages 114ff.

3. Luke 23:34.

4. 1 Corinthians 13:4.

5. Revelation 21:1.

### These Who Darken Counsel

1. Job 38:1–7, with verses 34–41 optional, is the Old Testament lesson listed during the season of Pentecost as Proper 24, year B, in the *RCL*.

2. Mark 10:35–45 is the New Testament lesson listed during the season of Pentecost as Proper 24, year B, in the *RCL*.

3. This character is based on a composite of two members of a congregation I served earlier in my career. Neither person is named Walenczky. All the details attributed to Mr. Walenczky are compatible with either and both of the persons on whom this fictitious person is based.

4. Like Mr. Walenczky, this character is a composite. All details are, however, drawn from the lives of real people, and all are compatible with each person who inspired the character. None is named Margaret Benjamin.